Unbeatable Mind

MAYA YOSHIDA

Unbeatable Mind

HarperCollins*Publishers*

HarperCollins*Publishers*
1 London Bridge Street
London SE1 9GF

www.harpercollins.co.uk

First published by HarperCollins*Publishers* 2018

1 3 5 7 9 10 8 6 4 2

© Maya Yoshida 2018

Maya Yoshida asserts the moral right to
be identified as the author of this work

A catalogue record of this book is
available from the British Library

ISBN 978-0-00-828933-1

Printed and bound in Great Britain by
CPI Group (UK) Ltd, Croydon, CR0 4YY

MIX
Paper from
responsible sources
FSC® C007454

This book is produced from independently certified FSC paper
to ensure responsible forest management.

For more information visit: www.harpercollins.co.uk/green

CONTENTS

INTRODUCTION

On 24 August 2017 I opened a new chapter in my life as a Southampton player when I signed a new three-year contract with the club.

I felt rejuvenated. On Southampton's official website the announcement of my new contract was accompanied by a photo of me with Mr Les Reed, the club's vice chairman, smiling and shaking each other's hand.

In truth, the vice chairman and my agent had been locked in a heated discussion until the very last minute in our final negotiation, which was supposed to be a formality, and my presence was required 'only to sign on the dotted line', according to my agent. Sitting next to him, I was actually thinking, 'This is so not what I expected …', although I also have to admit that a situation like this is not unusual in the world of professional football. Business is business.

The three-month-long negotiation came to a conclusion and a new contract, which had always been the first priority for both the club and myself, was finally agreed. It was, in fact, my second new contract here at this club on the

1

south coast of England. I was delighted that I could continue my journey as a Southampton player and try to better myself through all the challenges we continued to face together. Not only signing, but also announcing the new contract on my 29th birthday, was the best present I could possibly have asked for.

Playing in the Premier League had been my dream ever since I made up my mind to become a professional footballer in my early teens. It was also one of the goals I was audacious enough to believe would eventually be achieved. With the 2017/18 season being the sixth in my Premier League career, I honestly feel, as I said through the club's website when my new contract was announced, 'Southampton is my home.' That was my sincere first thought.

Then I received another 'offer', this time from a British publisher. It was shortly after I began my sixth Premier League season as a Southampton centre-back, resolved to make it the fifth consecutive top-10 finish for the club. In England the summer transfer window for a player usually closes at the end of August. The market is always open for authors, though, and I had no reason not to listen to what they had to offer.

The offer was, as it turned out, from one of the major publishers in the United Kingdom. Just by taking a quick look at their authors' list in the sports non-fiction category, I could see all those big names, including David Beckham and Frank Lampard, with whom I had dreamed to be on the same field when I was a kid. And now, here was an opportunity to put my name onto the same list as them.

Even though the book was explained to me as a joint project with the publisher's Japan office, to my Japanese mind it felt like I would become the author of a 'foreign book'. It is true that it has been more than eight years since I moved abroad, so I am used to being away from Japan. I could add that I am now quite comfortable communicating in English. As an author, I already have some experience publishing my books in my native country and, at one time, even joked that I rather fancied a quality post-playing life living on my book royalties. But still, publishing a book in English in the United Kingdom sounded a 'tough ask' to me. It was as if I would have the Premier League of publishing to prove myself in, as well as the real Premier League.

Then an editor at the publisher said to me, 'Don't worry. You have resilience, Maya!'

'Ri-zi-li-ens?' I couldn't even spell the word in my head at first. There seem to be various meanings in Japanese for this word, such as *gyakkyo-ryoku* (capacity to recover from adversity), *orenai-kokoro* (unbroken mind), *fukugen-ryoku* (ability to spring back into shape) or *taikyu-ryoku* (durability).

My interpretation is *makenai-chikara* – strength of unbeatable mind.

Bingo! As soon as this interpretation came to my mind, a light bulb was switched on brightly in my head (in the head of Maya Yoshida the author, I should say) because this particular strength is the essence of 'Maya power'. That's the quality that has carried me through, all the way from my childhood to the present day as a Premier League defender, striving to improve to reach a higher standard, sometimes feeling low in a tough environment, sometimes having luck on my side to break through, via the city of Nagoya in Japan and of Venlo in the Netherlands, all the way to Southampton.

Until I received this publishing opportunity, I'd never said this English word 'resilience' out loud but it has always been inside me, I realised. The more I thought about it, the more I became sure of it. I also started to believe that I could convey my feelings, thoughts and stories well enough to readers in both the United Kingdom and Japan through a book, if it had 'resilience' as its underlying theme.

Needless to say, writing a book itself is not easy. I like writing, but finishing a book under the pressure of an approaching deadline is another matter. I was sure that I would sometimes need to fight off drowsiness as I sat in front of my computer. But I was also sure that my 'strength of unbeatable mind' would once again carry me through this new challenge.

It was a huge opportunity that I could not and should not miss – to make my début in the field of English publishing at the top level. There was no time to hesitate, I decided in the end.

Yes, let's do this! I made one of the biggest decisions of my life. Well, that may be exaggerating a bit, but nonetheless I signed on a publishing contract that was also put in front of me at the beginning of my sixth year at Southampton.

There was one specific request from the publisher's Japan office about the direction of this book. They wanted me to see myself as a samurai, a warrior of a high social rank in eleventh- to nineteenth-century Japan, but with a size-five football at my feet instead of a shiny sword in my hands. So, to be more precise, the theme of the book should be 'samurai resilience'.

My initial reaction to this was that there seemed to be a slight difference between what Western people think of as a samurai and what we Japanese do. When I think of a samurai, what comes to my mind is someone prepared, if necessary, to kill himself by committing an act of *hara-*

kiri – cutting his stomach open to die in order to avoid dishonour.

On the other hand, I am under the impression that people in Europe see a samurai in the image of a true warrior: a brave fighter who never gives up and keeps on going till the very end. It is an image of someone with incredible toughness, whose every deed is fortified by resilience. This Western view of a samurai, as I understand it, is also quite different from someone who loves cracking jokes, the image I project in the 'Maya world', if I may call it that – the world I have depicted in my blog and previous books.

In the football world, a defender, especially a centre-back, can be an easy target for criticism because a single mistake made in 90 minutes could cost the game for his team. Some might say it is a thankless position because a centre-back won't be in the spotlight as often as a striker is but will be criticised for one costly mistake, even if it was made after 89 minutes and 59 seconds of an otherwise faultless performance. It may be true and I won't deny it. But to me, getting criticised is part of the job as a professional defender.

My experience as a centre-back, good and bad, makes me appreciate even more all the support and encouragement I have received over the years. I cannot thank everyone enough. I know people sometimes feel frustrated, or even gutted, after watching my performance, but you 'Maya supporters' still cheer me no matter what. That unconditional support has strengthened the unbeatable mind that I have.

If I succeed in passing on some seed of resilience that I have found in my life so far to my supporters, or to people who have picked up this book because of their passion for Southampton FC, the Japan national football team, the Premier League or football itself, I will be a happy author.

Resilience can give you strength to keep moving forwards when you are caught in the rain or a storm, and keep you continuing on your journey through life. And it is a strength that resides in everyone. If you come to realise that, it will be a reward that I genuinely treasure as the author of this book.

CHAPTER 1

YOUNGEST SON RISING

The origin: strength of the youngest

If I am to talk about resilience, I must start with my child-hood in a city called Nagasaki where I was born, on the island of Kyushu located about 600 miles south-west of Tokyo. That is because one of the resilient traits I was born with is the 'strength of the youngest'. I can hear some people saying, 'What?' and I certainly understand that there is no such definition for the word 'resilience' in any available dictionaries. But believe me, 'strength of the youngest' is a definition to be found in the dictionary of Maya Yoshida.

I started playing football for fun just before I was enrolled at a Japanese elementary school (Year 1 to Year 7 in the UK). I was the youngest of three brothers in my family and started playing in a kickabout with my two brothers and their friends. The J.League (Japan Professional Football League) started when I was around five years old, and was initially just a single division – although it has since grown to have three tiers. My brothers, who were already in their impressionable early teens by then, totally immersed themselves in the 'soccer boom' sweeping through the country, triggered by the creation of the much-anticipated domestic professional league.

All my brothers did whenever they had free time was play football. It was football during the lunch break, football after school and football at the weekend. Naturally, that meant it was the same for their youngest brother. It was football day in, day out for me, too. In my mind, having fun meant kicking a ball with them.

The city of Nagasaki back then didn't have a local club in the J.League, so I didn't really have a chance to watch a professional football game at a stadium. My sole live experience was when Verdy Kawasaki (now called Tokyo Verdy 1969) came to a town called Isahaya located in the middle of Nagasaki Prefecture for a game. If my memory serves me right, it was a game in the Emperor's Cup (similar to the FA Cup here in England), not a league game, but I still remember the excitement I felt in the stand on that day, watching a professional football game right in front of me for the first time in my life.

I didn't follow any particular club or players when I was a kid. I was more a big fan of football itself, especially playing the game. In most parts of Japan baseball is the number one professional sport. However, it wasn't because football was particularly popular in Kyushu that

I was drawn to the game. There were kids playing base-ball, too, in my neighbourhood.

Having said that, maybe it was significant that there wasn't a baseball team in my elementary school, but there was a football team. Hmmm, I guess I was fortu-nate to be born in a football-friendly environment. Anyway, what I wanted to say was that football was around me for as long as I can remember and playing football was just a natural thing for me to do to have fun as a kid.

However, there was one problem. The lads I always enjoyed a kickabout with were my brothers and their friends. I'm seven years younger than my oldest brother and six years younger than the other one. It meant that, even though I was big for an elementary-school boy, there was no way for me to compete physically with them when they were already going to junior high school (Year 8 to Year 10).

I was always the tallest among my classmates. I was 5' 6" when I was 12, about six inches taller than the national average for that age. I remember also that I shot up to a little over 5' 10" in the following 12 months. But I must have been only just above four foot tall when I started playing football and I could easily be brushed aside by my brothers and their friends, who were nearly a foot taller than me. So it was only natural for me to try to outsmart the boys who were physically stronger than I was, and try to play clever in order to compete with the much bigger lads. This way of thinking was always with me from the very earliest stage of my development as a footballer.

I was always good with the ball, too, whether it was kicking or controlling it. Yes, the youngest son of the Yoshida family has always had what it takes to be a 'player', although he was destined to be a defender. Thankfully, my brothers didn't really come charging at me, their little brother, at full tilt when I was on the ball. That allowed me a bit of freedom on the playground to express myself, trying to beat an opponent who was bigger than me by being clever or technical, and the fact I could show off my skills made me fall in love with football even more. Maybe that's why if I have to name one boyhood hero of mine, it would be Dragan Stojković, also known by his nickname 'Piksi', who delighted the J.League crowds while I was growing up with his incredible skills in an attacking midfield role at Nagoya Grampus Eight.

Later in my development, when I started watching games from a defender's point of view, Rio Ferdinand became one of the players that I most admired. The former Manchester United defender had much more success in his football career than his brother Anton, who is seven years younger than him. Among the former Man United defenders, there were the Neville brothers, too. Again, the achievements of older brother Gary overshadow those of the younger brother Phil, in terms of the number of trophies and medals won. But I, for one, believe that a 'football career favours the youngest', if such a proverb exists.

I say this because if you are the youngest brother or sister, you tend to play football with someone older, such as your siblings or their friends. That makes you aware of your particular weakness right from the start, whether it is a smaller physique or slower pace, and as a result you sometimes have to endure pain and frustration. But those experiences will toughen you up both physically and mentally, and also can lead you to compensate for your shortcomings in order to beat or stop your opponent, who is stronger or better in some departments. Therefore the youngest, in the end, has more chance to improve as a footballer and surpass his or her elders, who might have found it easy to get the better of someone younger or smaller, without having to make any extra effort, when they were young. That's what I think, anyway.

I didn't know it until I started writing this book, but John Terry, the former Chelsea centre-back, is an example of my belief – the younger of two brothers turned out to be more successful as a footballer. I don't really know him personally, but from purely a centre-back's point of view it is not bad, I think, to follow the same pattern as him, a defender whom I looked up to, together with the likes of Ferdinand, throughout my development as a footballer.

Eyes of the youngest

The two older brothers of the Yoshida family weren't born to pursue a career as a professional footballer. Even though, as their brother, I look at them through rose-tinted glasses, I must say they weren't good enough. My older brother had stopped playing by the time he was 16. The oldest one carried on playing in his high-school years (age 16 to 18) but only as a back-up goalkeeper.

If there was one thing that made me feel, 'I'm no different to my brothers,' it was my name, Maya. Even though I was the only one among the football-loving Yoshida brothers to go on to become a professional, I could not avoid the fate of being given a female-sounding name. My oldest brother is named Honami, while the older one is called Mirei. Both names sound feminine to Japanese ears. My dad was desperate for a daughter, I was told, and that may explain the names our parents chose for us.

It's not as though I didn't like my name when I was a kid. It was more a case of being annoyed by people so often ridiculing me, saying, 'You have a girl's name!', and especially by repeatedly having to say, 'I'm not a girl,' whenever someone called my name for the first time.

For instance, at the beginning of a school year, when a new teacher checked attendance by calling everyone's name in the class, when it was my turn the call would come, 'Yoshida Maya-chan?' (In Japanese, it's always the surname first, and 'chan' is usually added for a girl to make it sound friendly.) When this happened, which was almost every time, I would answer, 'Yes, I'm here, but I'm a boy.' It was the same when I went to a hospital or the dentist's. A nurse would call out, 'Yoshida Maya-chan,' and I would reply, 'I'm not a girl, but it's me!' The only good thing that came out of these experiences was that I managed to develop immunity to being teased by people around me from a very young age.

But today I'm glad that I was called Maya. I really want to thank my parents for giving me that name, as it is one that seems easy not only to remember but also to pronounce for a non-Japanese as well.

Here in the United Kingdom, people tend to give a player a nickname with the letter 's' or 'y' or 'ie' at the end of it, to make it easier to call out during a game, such as 'Lamps', 'Giggsy' or 'Stevie'. But I have always been called by my real name, 'Maya', including during my time in the Netherlands before my move to Southampton. (Once in a while, a Saints fan would shout 'Yoshi!' to get my attention, and I was probably annoyingly slow to react as I'm not used to being called by that name ...)

Anyhow, Maya-chan, with a female-sounding name but with a bigger than average body, was a clever elementary-school kid, I must say. I excelled at sports in general and wasn't too bad academically as well. I wasn't the smartest in my class but wasn't one of those who would get scolded by the teacher for their poor grades either. I was very good at dealing with things at school without trying my hardest. It was only after entering junior high school that I changed my attitude, resolving to do my best in whatever I do. Until then I was able to take it easy in most of the things I did at school.

The fact that Maya-chan managed to avoid becoming conceited is pretty much down to my brothers and their friends. Having them around me was like being surrounded by role models. Through my observation of older people around me, I could pick up some of their good habits, thinking, 'This must be the way to do it,' or 'I shall follow his example.' I became very good at doing precisely that.

Watching them, I sometimes told myself, 'I shouldn't do that,' or 'I can't be like that,' using them as a bad example. People used to call me a precocious brat when I was a kid, and it was true in a way, as I often coolly observed my brothers and their friends from a step or two away. And that I think became the foundation of my ability to look at things objectively from a neutral perspective.

Even from a young age, while watching people around me rather matter-of-factly, I was always thinking in my head, 'What would I do?' 'How can I be like that?' 'What should I do if I don't want to be like that?' This particular way of looking at things became more and more important and useful as I continued my development as a footballer, especially after I became a professional player, as it turned out.

When I was struggling to get playing time at Southampton, I often said to journalists in the mixed zone, a designated area at a stadium (often near a team coach pick-up point) for the media to get post-match quotes from players, 'I understand where I am in the team right now. I just need to keep on working hard, doing what I have to do.' Looking back now, I think I was able to say that because of this inner strength of mine which developed from an early age as the youngest brother, the strength of mind to face up to reality.

My brothers had shown me so much that ensured this precocious brat of their little brother wouldn't become a cocky king of the hill. They had also made me try many things that seemed impossible for me to accomplish. Applying for the Nagoya Grampus Eight academy was one of those. At first, it was only to remind me of the danger of becoming a big fish in a small pond.

A small fish in a bigger pond

In my elementary-school days I never felt that I'd be beaten in a game at the local level. In fact, I hardly lost an individual battle on the pitch back in those days. I played in the school team at Sako Elementary School (which later became Nanryo FC), not at Nita Elementary School which I was actually going to, because the latter only allowed pupils in the third year or above to be in the team there. Besides, the two schools were located just a stone's throw away from each other.

Sako wasn't a school known for its strong football team so we seldom went into a tournament at the prefecture level, let alone the national level. In addition, I wasn't especially keen to play in an official school match or tournament, as I had no aspiration to be a professional footballer whatsoever while at elementary school and was just playing for fun at that time. There really was a danger of me becoming living proof that the frog in the well knows nothing of the great ocean, a player who was merely happy to be invincible in a local school football world.

Possibly sensing that danger, my oldest brother, who was living by himself in Fukuoka, a city along the north shore of Kyushu island, sent me an application form for a youth academy trial when I was in my last year at elementary school, thinking I would need a tougher challenge to broaden my horizons.

It just so happened to be the one in Nagoya, a city in the middle of mainland Japan. He'd googled for a youth academy at J.League clubs while looking online for information about a university for which he was going to take an entrance exam, and the only trial calling for applications at that time was the one at the Grampus youth academy.

He never thought I would pass the trial. Everyone around me thought I had no chance, and so did I.

There were 60 or 70 participants on the day of the trial, I think, and four were successful, including myself. Being a boy from a small town in Kyushu, I'd imagined there would be hundreds of kids trialling with a J.League club, so when I saw the actual number that turned up I thought, 'This is it? Much less than I imagined.' Maybe that carefree attitude helped me to go through, and this 'big fish' from Nagasaki ended up going to the 'bigger pond' that was Nagoya.

I was only 12 at that time. I have heard many people saying, 'It was such a brave decision to leave home at such a young age.' I still do. People tell me that it was as courageous, if not more so, as the decision I made to move abroad when I was 21. But to be honest, the 12-year-old Maya Yoshida didn't think he had made such a huge decision. It was more like, 'I can always come back home after a year or two if it doesn't work out.' I was that casual about joining the youth academy in Nagoya.

Given that he was the one who'd sent the life-changing application form to his little brother, my oldest brother may have felt somewhat concerned when I ended up leaving home at the age of 12. But I wasn't feeling any pressure or responsibility at all, even when it was time to leave Nagasaki.

However, something changed inside me once I arrived in Nagoya. I started feeling the pressure that comes from realising there would be no way for me to go home without achieving anything. I needed to rent a flat to start my life in Nagoya. We also had to buy some basic furniture. In Japan, a flat to let generally means unfurnished. Even a 12-year-old could understand it was costing the Yoshida household good money. The fact that my parents had to spend money because I was joining the academy in a different part of Japan made me think that I could not give up too easily and go back to Nagasaki after only a year or two. Initially, it was more a case of me feeling that I owed it to my parents to persevere than wanting to meet the expectations of my family. I felt strongly that I just could not go home with nothing to show for their financial sacrifices, and that sense of responsibility turned, in the end, into an inner determination to knuckle down to becoming a professional footballer.

Looking back now, I can't help but wonder how my parents let their youngest son leave home for a city some 400 miles away at that age. I really want to tell them, 'It was a brave decision.' Even though Kyushu and mainland Japan are connected by a bridge and an undersea tunnel, to a 12-year-old boy from Nagasaki it was like going to live in a foreign land. I actually flew over to Nagoya. Now I'm a father myself, I can't imagine letting my daughter go to live in a city away from home when she is only 12 or 13.

However, it wasn't the case that my parents didn't care much about letting their youngest son leave home. The plan was that I would live with my cousin's family in Aichi Prefecture, of which Nagoya is the capital city. That was part of the reason why I was so casual about leaving home; I assumed, 'I can go to the academy from their home.' It was only on the day I was leaving for Nagoya accompanied by my mum, already on the plane and in the air, that she told me about 'something important'. I found out that living with my cousin's family was no longer an option due to an unforeseeable circumstance at their end. You can imagine my surprise. I was lost for words, except 'What?!'

At that time, both my mum and dad were working in Nagasaki, and my older brother had just left for Tokyo to go to university. That meant my oldest brother, who was also away but just preparing to take the entrance exam (equivalent of A-level exams in the UK) again, had to come to my rescue to live with me in Nagoya. It was very last minute and so not according to the original plan. But on the other hand, this unexpected development made it easier for me, in a way, to make up my mind to go to Nagoya, as there was no other choice; I had to accept the reality.

So I left my home for Nagoya, where a different kind of resilience from 'the strength of the youngest' would be nurtured.

Anti-complex power

The junior youth (aged 12 to 15) set-up at Grampus was at a totally different level from what I was used to in Nagasaki. The moment I joined its Under-12/13 team, I felt a sense of urgency. Watching other players around me, I was shocked at how good they were. They all seemed way ahead of me, and the exceptionally good ones were invited to train with a team in the age group above us. There were four such players in my age group, and I secretly called them 'the Big Four'. As for me, I was starting from the absolute bottom in the youth ranks. Every day I could not help but feel, 'I have to get past every one of them, including the Big Four.'

We all got on well as team-mates but we were in competition to climb up the ladder in the academy. So I had to make sure that I wouldn't be just one of the crowd but a force to be reckoned with through my performances.

It was as if the world I had read about in football *manga* (Japanese comics) was there right in front of me as the reality.

Every time I made a step forwards, to reach a higher level or rank, there came new rivals. As soon as I thought I had beaten my competition, there was another rival to beat. I tried to keep on running, but hurdles kept on appearing in my path.

The biggest motivation for me when I started out in the academy at Grampus, realising for the first time how fierce the competition would be within the team, was the awareness that I simply could not go back to Nagasaki without giving it proper time. And the fact that I managed to overcome the initial pressure was, I believe, down to my nature. I hate losing. I don't want to be a loser in whatever I do, so I turn the sense of urgency which comes from thinking 'I can't lose' into positive energy to reach my goal, instead of merely putting even more pressure onto myself. That is how I keep on running this long hurdle race that is the career of a footballer.

I wasn't a prodigy or an elite youth player who had been developed at the academy of a professional club from the age of six or seven. I was just a kid who played football in a local school team, and I had something of an 'I-am-a-nobody' complex when I joined the Grampus academy. So when I saw other academy players, part of me was simply impressed by their abilities while another part was thinking, 'I don't want to lose against them no matter what.' It was the same when I got my first call-up to the national youth team or the Japan senior side. I always had this 'me against the elites' feeling inside me.

I believe there are many people with a similar complex around the world, including in Japan and the United Kingdom. I also believe it is possible for anyone to deal with such a feeling of inferiority in a positive way. Thinking that you don't want to be beaten by it gives you mental strength – 'anti-complex power', if I may call it that. And that is certainly a part of the resilience that has helped this Japanese defender end up plying his trade in the Premier League.

By mental strength, I don't mean something that only a spiritual seeker can master, as though a professional athlete must become a practitioner of stoicism or asceticism. I did try to stay away from snacking and drinking fizzy drinks in my early teens, but what seems equally important to me nowadays, as a professional footballer, in order to develop or use my resilience is being able to switch oneself on and off effectively in one's daily life. It is more important if you play abroad because you are likely to spend more time by yourself than when you are in your native country, especially right after your transfer to a different country, where thinking about football, about what you should or shouldn't do as a player all the time, might lead to being too hard on yourself and have a negative effect on you, especially as you are under pressure to perform straight away.

Fortunately, I have always been quite good at dealing with life. Even after a defeat or poor individual performance, I rarely feel down once I'm home. I know when I must be switched on and when I can switch myself off as a footballer. There is always something else to take my mind away from football if needed. I'm innately curious; I've always been that way.

For instance, when I moved from Nagasaki to Nagoya and realised that there was a tough road ahead at the academy for me, it wasn't as though I couldn't think about or do anything other than football. My junior high-school days were not only about football. It was the time when a *manga* titled *BECK* was popular in Japan, and I wanted to have the same electric guitar – a telecaster – that the main character played in the story.

Of course I begged and begged my oldest brother, who at the time was also my guardian, to buy me one. One day, after two hours of my begging and his refusal, and getting fed up with each other (it was, I have to admit now, a case of little brother behaving badly), he finally gave in and bought me the guitar I wanted. Needless to say, I was grinning from ear to ear, hugging my precious instrument and snuggling up to my brother sitting next to me on our train journey home. On Mondays, I sometimes enjoyed playing the guitar with my friends after school as there was no team training at the academy.

At the moment, Maya Yoshida the guitarist is in semi-retirement, or has been forced to be so, to be more precise. My guitar has been locked away somewhere in our house so that there is no chance of my baby daughter knocking it down by accident and harming herself. Might I need some resilience to fight off an occasional urge to take out the guitar and play? Probably not. Maya Yoshida the husband and father gladly takes a back seat to his beloved wife and daughter.

High school is hell

As Maya Yoshida the footballer, I basically don't want to be behind anyone. I don't want to feel inferior to anybody. And that is why I chose to go to a prefectural high school (age 16 to 18), instead of going to an independent one that was in partnership with the club, even though I was already determined to be a professional footballer by then.

My attitude towards becoming a professional had changed gradually over the course of three years in junior high school. First, I only thought, 'I should at least give it a real go.' Then I started to feel, 'I really want to be a professional.' And in the end, I simply thought, 'I'll be a professional footballer,' without any doubts.

But pursuing a career as a footballer also made me aware of another anxiety I had inside me. I always thought that people might see me as a boy who wouldn't be able do anything properly apart from playing football because I'd left home early and wasn't under the guidance of my parents from a young age. I felt I had to do something to change that perception, for I would hate to be seen that way.

Tuition is much cheaper at a prefectural school. My mum used to tell me in a light-hearted fashion, 'You go to a state school because an independent school is too expensive for us.' But my going there was mainly because of my determination to stop people viewing me in a negative way. I didn't want them saying, 'Maya lacks common sense because all he has done is to play football,' or 'Maya can't do anything else,' so I decided to go to a prefectural high school, even if it meant I had to study for the entrance exam (the equivalent of GSCE in the UK). I just couldn't accept the idea that I might be labelled as someone who would be useless and worthless apart from his ability at football.

I passed the exam and enrolled at Toyota Senior High School. I'd succeeded in what I set out to do but felt miserable right away. As soon as my high-school life began, I felt as though I couldn't continue. The first thing my form teacher said was, 'There's never been a professional footballer or baseball player from this school.' I understood that this was intended to encourage me, and other students, to study hard so that we might go on to university or college, but it still felt like I had been dealt a major setback from the get-go. I remember thinking as the teacher spoke, 'You'll be eating your words some day.'

My team-mates at the Grampus academy were all going to the club-affiliated private high school, which was much closer to the club's residence hall. I, too, had moved in there after finishing junior high school, but I was going to a different high school. So I had to get up earlier than anyone in the team to start a 30-minute bike ride there every day, sometimes against the elements.

My time at the school was even harder. Although I knew it would be the case, being a youth player at Grampus meant nothing to the teachers and I wasn't treated any differently to the other students, including in the amount of homework I was given. I got tons.

Moreover, they had very strict regulations. Given that the school's academic standard was roughly the same as the region's other state schools, the idea perhaps was to keep the students disciplined to prevent them from falling into pitfalls that might have enticed and trapped them under a more relaxed regime. But it was a very strict environment. I really felt I had arrived in hell once I enrolled there.

In my first year I hardly spoke to any of my classmates. I spent most of the time between classes napping at my desk rather than chatting, and my lunchtimes were spent with a close friend from my junior high school days. I wasn't always a good communicator, as people (might) think today after watching me on the football pitch. Anyway, taking into account the type of school it was and my difficulties fitting in there, I thought, 'I've f***** up my school choice.'

By the way, at Southampton, where I have happily settled in, academy players study after their morning training session. They take online courses, instead of going to a local school. In Japan, everything is done by the club to help the young player finish their compulsory education curriculum. This may mean that an academy player in Japan ends up more academically advanced than one here. However, I personally think the English way offers a good and practical educational system for a kid who gives priority to his football education, especially for someone who is determined to pursue a professional career from a very young age.

I also think that, over here, it is much more common to steer your own course from a young age than in Japan. That is one of the key differences I have noticed since moving to Europe. In the United Kingdom, for instance, teenagers seem to be given the chance to decide which subjects to study further, based on their particular interests or their intended future career. They start making decisions about their own lives from a young age and do so constantly as they grow up.

How about in Japan? Most young people there, it seems to me, don't make many decisions concerning the path they intend to follow until they are around 20 years of age. Once you finish your compulsory education you go to a high school, and then take an entrance exam to get into a university or college. As long as you study adequately, you can go up to a certain point, as if you are on an escalator, where you see multiple routes open up in front of you. But at the same time you may also see that you aren't especially prepared to take any of the routes available to you. It could be said that you have a well-rounded education, but you have achieved almost nothing outstanding.

English and me

Despite feeling as though I was in hell at my high school, one subject I was enthusiastic about was English. I studied very hard because I wanted to. I was never an academic high-flier, but I'm proud of the eagerness I showed to learn English.

Why English? Well, again, it has something to do with my complex – an inferiority complex towards anything foreign. When I was a teenager, I always felt that cultural imports from abroad – whether English pop and rock music, or the latest fashions from Europe or the United States – were better and much cooler than the things I saw or heard in Japan.

At that time, I was living in a place that was essentially a commuter town for people working in the city of Toyota. Naturally, I was surrounded by so-called 'third-culture kids' – children who'd come back from abroad where their fathers worked as expatriates at overseas branches or affiliated companies of the Toyota Motor Corporation, in the case of the town I was living in. At my school, it was nothing unusual to find a student or two in the class who, let's say, had just come back from the west coast of the United States or had visited several countries while in Europe. I could sense something different about those kids, a scent of foreign culture, and I was attracted to it. In my mind, anything foreign was extremely cool and the English language expressed that coolness verbally. That's how I initially got into the language when I was a junior high-school student.

Then, at high school, I decided that English was an essential subject. My desire to play football abroad had developed into something like a plan for my future by the time I became a high-school student. 'To go abroad, English is a must as a communication tool,' I thought. So I studied it really seriously.

I can't say I did anything special or extra apart from attending my English classes. Unlike during my previous three years at junior high school, I didn't have much energy or time left after spending the day at school and then at the club for football training. But at least I tried to put 120 per cent into my English class. I did my best to learn English grammar and to increase my vocabulary without falling asleep ('You can't call that a big effort,' some might say ...).

I know grammar and vocabulary aren't everything when it comes to learning a foreign language, but in any language, including my native Japanese tongue, if your grasp of its grammar and vocabulary is poor, your writing and speaking will lack clarity, as you will end up repeatedly using similar and awkward expressions. I didn't want to be like that when it came to moving abroad, so, to me, getting the basics of English grammar and vocabulary right in my high-school years was very important.

In terms of having a conversation in English, I was nowhere near being able to do that at the time. There was a class for listening and speaking at school, but I didn't find it very practical or useful. At Grampus there were some foreign coaches and foreign first-team players, but none of them were English natives. I had heard that watching English movies without Japanese subtitles could be a good way to improve one's listening comprehension, but I found that too frustrating. Besides lacking patience, I was also short of the stamina required, after a day's school and youth-team training, to sit through another 90 minutes or so of watching a movie that I couldn't really understand.

But I was training my English ears a little by listening to the American or British music that I loved. Again, it's not like I made an extra effort, such as trying to remember the lyrics or to understand the words with a dictionary in my hand; I'd simply been getting used to hearing English in this way since my early teens. In my high-school days I remember listening to songs by an American band called Maroon 5, whose popularity rose in Japan at that time. I also liked the music of rock or blues gods such as Aerosmith or Eric Clapton, though I tended to go for slower, mellower tunes, such as their ballads, as it was easier for me to catch some of the words in the lyrics.

It was at this time that Sugao Kambe and the late Che Hyon Pak helped me to see England as the ultimate destination in my football life. They came to the Grampus academy as coaches from another J.League club called Jef United Ichiahara Chiba when I was 16. Mr Kambe had more of a directorial role; Mr Pak spent most of his time coaching us, and so was key in helping me to become a Japanese centre-back playing abroad.

Under the new coach, we started – or were ordered, I should say – to watch Premier League games on DVD as part of our football education. Watching matches involving clubs like Liverpool or Chelsea, I couldn't help but be super-impressed. The fans were so noisy, I could feel the atmosphere inside the stadiums through the TV screen! When a goal was scored, I could feel the passion of the fans as they went nuts.

Watching these matches, I immediately wanted to play in England, and somehow I soon came to believe, 'That's where I will play.' It was typical of me; my innate optimism and self-belief have, I believe, helped me every step along the way to get to where I am now.

It was Mr Pak who converted me back to a defensive midfielder. Defensive midfielder? Convert back? Yes, that's right. Maya Yoshida wasn't a natural-born centre-back.

Pre-centre-back era

When I started to play football for fun, I was kicking the ball as if I was a *fantasista* on the pitch. Everybody did so as a kid, I believe, and I was no exception. I was playing as a striker or a number 10, a star role in my team when I was little. I had no inkling whatsoever of my suitability as a defender. I never ever thought, 'I'd be good as a defender.' Even when I watched a game of football, my eyes were drawn to attacking players.

I think it is particularly the case with my generation that, as kids, we preferred playing behind the striker and setting up a goal rather than actually scoring as a forward. We had grown up reading a hugely popular football *manga* titled 'Captain Tsubasa' (a modern Japanese version of the Roy of the Rovers cartoon strip character over here). I was one of numerous Japanese football kids who wanted to play the number 10 role, just as the main character, Tsubasa, did in the *manga*. When in a one-on-one situation with a goalkeeper, I would rather square the ball nonchalantly for my onrushing team-mate to score than beat the goalie and score myself. That was cool, like Tsubasa, and I loved it.

However, as I grew up and climbed the ladder towards a professional career, my position on the pitch moved further and further back. Now playing as a centre-back, there is only a goalkeeper left behind me. But until I reached around 14 years of age, towards the end of my second year at junior high school, I was a central midfielder. And when Mr Pak became a coach at the Grampus academy he put me back in the middle of the pitch.

Recently, I had a chance to join Kei Yamaguchi, a former defensive midfielder and my senior from my Grampus days at a football clinic held in Japan, and there I discovered that even he and many other seniors at the club thought I'd come up through the youth ranks as a centre-back. Little did they know that I became a professional footballer as a central midfielder.

People see me solely as a centre-back these days, but in my mind I'm always a former midfielder. I believe my experience in an anchor-man role helped me to make a great leap during my youth development. I even think that I couldn't have become a professional if I hadn't spent my final two years in the youth team (age 16 to 18) as a defensive midfielder. That is how strongly I feel about the importance to me – in terms of my career – of having formerly been a midfielder.

The fact that I'm comfortable with my allegedly weaker left foot, a trait more common among midfielders than defenders, however, has more to do with the fact that I've always tried to be two-footed since I was a kid. In my elementary-school days I used to practise using a slope near my home. I kicked a ball up from the bottom of the slope and when the ball was rolling down back I controlled it and kicked it again. I repeated this over and over again, using my right and left foot in turn.

My background as a defensive midfielder still influences how I play today. As a centre-back, when I have to deal with the ball either with my foot or my head, I usually try to check my team-mates' positions around me and make a pass rather than a mere clearance, if possible. That awareness of space and the position of a team-mate comes from being a defensive midfielder.

I also know from experience that it will be really tough for a defensive midfielder if a clearance by a centre-back gives the ball straight back to the opponents. My team-mates' workload depends on whether or not we can build up from the back line after stopping the opponent's attack. If I can feed the ball to a team-mate, it gives the whole team time to move forwards rather than retreating to defend again.

That's just a small part of what we defenders do but it's the sort of detail that can make a huge difference in terms of how a game goes and how tired team-mates become. When I started watching games on DVD, I real-ised that good Premier League players always care about such details. Those viewing sessions were very beneficial for someone like me, adept at learning simply through observation.

Players I admired – and hugely optimistically started looking forward to playing with on the same pitch, whether as a team-mate or an opponent – were also mainly midfielders, such as Steven Gerrard, Frank Lampard or Claude Makélélé. Gerrard and Lampard were especially influential for me. I thought they were a class apart even among the other accomplished Premier League players of that era.

Playing in central midfield gives you a different view of the pitch from the one you get in the middle of the defensive line. As a centre-back, your view is basically locked in on what is going on ahead of you, while as a central midfielder you need a much wider range of vision. You get pressure from your opponents from the side or behind as well as in front. At first, when playing in that role, there were times when the ball was nicked off me by someone whom I wasn't paying enough attention to. But once you get used to playing in the middle of the pitch, you start enjoying it more, too. I felt it was fun to initiate an attack from a deep-lying position. Also, it felt good every time I sniffed danger and stopped the opponent's attack before it actually developed.

In midfield, I also found that I could polish what I had been trying to equip myself to do since I started kicking a ball with my brothers and their friends, such as developing complete control of the ball and learning to think quickly in order to beat older, more developed opponents. That, I think, is why Mr Pak put me back in midfield – to improve my technique and awareness.

Beginning of the long-distance hurdle race

The role I was given by Mr Pak in the Grampus youth team was that of anchor-man – a one-man shield for the back line. While I was learning and performing in that pivotal role between the team's attack and defence, I was also named team captain. My character – naturally positive but objective and realistic at the same time – no doubt contributed to me getting the armband.

By the end of the season I led the Grampus Under-18 team to just one win away from being crowned as the national champions in the 2006 Prince Takamado Trophy All Japan Youth Football League, in which professional clubs' youth sides competed with high-school football teams. That professional club involvement distinguished the tournament from the two other major domestic youth tournaments in Japan, namely the All Japan High School Soccer Tournament and the Inter High School Sports Festival (Football). In the tournament proper, 24 teams who came through regional qualifiers were divided into six groups of four in the first round, and then the top two teams in each group competed in the knockout stage to reach the summit of the Japanese domestic youth football world.

We lost to a team from Takigawa Dai-ni High School in the final, but my performance in the tournament as an anchor-man wearing the captain's armband didn't go unnoticed by my coaches. By then I had already occasionally been invited to first-team practice sessions at Grampus. I don't think my overall physical strength really stood out among my professional seniors, but I believe the coaches thought I was worth taking a closer look at in the first-team environment because of my height and ability to build up from the back. When I joined the academy at the age of 12, I was in awe of players around me such as the 'Big Four', the four team-mates who were regularly called up to join the team in the higher age group, but now I felt I had a chance of being promoted from the youth to the first team at Grampus.

It would be a lie if I said that, as a high-school student, I didn't feel uncomfortable or like an outsider when all the others in my class were thinking about going on to have a higher education while I was trying to set out on the path to becoming a professional footballer. But quitting school was never an option because I didn't want to be labelled as someone who could do nothing but football. At the same time, I didn't want to be viewed by people at the academy as a youth player who couldn't make it because he was going to a state school. I have always set myself targets that seemed difficult to reach.

At a J.League club, only a few players are given a professional contract at the end of the youth development process (at the age of 18). I have heard that only around 1 per cent of youth graduates at a Premier League club make it, but even in the J.League I reckon that only around 2 per cent of youth players go on to become a professional with their club. I, together with three other youth graduates, was given a professional contract by Grampus, and it was unprecedented in the club's history that four players from the youth academy were promoted to the first team as professionals at the same time.

In order to pass through such a narrow gate, it is important to have a clear vision of how you're going to reach a higher standard from an early stage in your development. How far you go depends to a large extent on how high you set your goal as well as the actions you take to reach it. I believe this applies not only to players at youth academies in Japan or at J.League clubs, but also to those playing in any league in any country. It could even be the same for players or competitors in other sports, or for those trying to work their way up in a corporation or organisation.

Of course, on your way to reaching your goal there may be times when you feel as though you've hit a wall; you feel inadequate or far behind the others. But you can't give up or lower your aspirations. You shouldn't swap the high hurdle in front of you for a lower one, imagining that this will make it easier to continue running. If you have the right mental attitude, a sense of inferiority or impending defeat can be turned into a positive energy, a boost to help you clear the hurdle or smash through the wall. That's how you get used to clearing hurdles one by one, barely noticing that each gets a little higher along the way. Certainly, that was how this youngest brother of three, who left his home town at the tender age of 12, managed to reach the point where, in my long-distance hurdle race towards a football career, I could see the starting line in terms of becoming a professional player.

CHAPTER 2

FIRST PROFESSIONAL VOYAGE

Survival instinct

In January 2007 I signed a professional contract with Nagoya Grampus Eight, and began my new challenge in the first team. It didn't mean I started to play immediately, though. I was only an 18-year-old former youth player there and I had to wait for about two months before making my first-team début. I wasn't even on the bench for the first two games of the season (the J.League season usually starts late in February or early March and ends in December in the same year). On the day of our opening game at home, I was instead helping the club off the pitch, dealing with ticket distribution before the match.

Back then, I just did whatever jobs I was given without questioning – even if it meant I would play a 'position' off the pitch. But now, I wonder if it was one of those typical old Japanese customs: regarding a young player automatically as an apprentice even if he had a professional contract. I don't think that would be the case here at Southampton. I believe the club treats such players as professionals once they have a professional contract regardless of their age, even if they are still in their teens.

In general, people over here in Europe focus on doing what they are supposed to be doing, whether they are footballers, office workers or shop staff. They tend to stick with doing what they are paid for under their contracts (although I have to admit that this tendency sometimes makes them look a bit too inflexible to me, as someone who is used to a meticulous level of Japanese customer service).

Having said that, I have no complaints whatsoever about the fact that the first-team opportunities for me were hard to come by at the beginning, because, to put it simply, I was around the bottom of the pecking order. I was a nobody from the youth ranks. Many of the players in the team didn't even know I'd been originally promoted as a defensive midfielder.

A team on the pitch consists of 11 players, of course. Even in a practice game on the training ground, there can only be a total of 22 players from the squad playing at the same time. And I couldn't even get into those 22 when I initially joined the first team. When I did eventually have a chance to participate in a practice game at the training ground, the position I played in depended on where numbers were short on that particular day. If it happened to be a centre-back position, I was put in the middle of the back line. If an extra defensive midfielder was needed, I played in the middle of the pitch to fill the vacancy.

There was another wall to break through, a bureaucratic one, in terms of becoming a recognised first-team player. Under the J.League regulations, there are three categories for a professional player under contract: Professional A, B and C. I could only be given a Professional C contract, the lowest category as a player with 450 minutes or less of total playing time in the J1 league (the top division in the J.League). And at our training centre, the dressing room for players with a C contract was separated from the one for players with contracts in higher categories.

I found the atmosphere in the dressing room for the C-contract players rather negative. I'd hear comments like 'I'm not in the team again!' or 'I should be playing rather than him because I'm better' coming from players who had found out that they were not in the starting 11 or who had failed to make the squad travelling to an away game. Watching those around me during the first month I spent there, and feeling that negative atmosphere in the dressing room, I remember starting to feel, 'I can't be stuck in here. I've got to say goodbye to this dressing room as soon as possible if I want to make it at the top level.' It was my survival instinct kicking in, urging me to do whatever I could to leave behind me a depressing environment that could have stagnated my professional career just when it had begun.

I tried my best to get closer to the A-contract players, approaching them off the pitch. Being the youngest of three brothers, I'm naturally used to being among my seniors, and was neither reluctant nor uncomfortable to share the company of those older than me. So yes, my resilience, 'strength of the youngest', helped me to make progress there. When we had lunch at the club's canteen after team training, I tried to mingle at a table where the first-team regulars were. I also had the temerity to occupy the back seat on the team coach when travelling.

In Japan, there is an unwritten rule at a football club, and in the national team set-up too, that the back seat of a team coach is reserved for 'VIPs' (Very Important Players). At Grampus in my time there, Toshiya-san (Toshiya Fujita) and Nara-san (Seigo Narazaki), who were both in their thirties, and Kei-kun (Kei Yamaguchi), who was in his sixth year in the first team, were the regular occupants of the back seats. ('San' is a Japanese honorific suffix added to either the surname or given name of a person to show respect to someone senior or among equals, while 'kun' is an honorific common among male friends.) For someone who had just come up from the youth team to sit in the back seat would definitely be going against the rule. But I realised there was always one more space available in the back seat on our team coach, so I summoned up my courage and sat there one day.

Once I was sitting with the 'VIPs', although they frequently made fun of this out-of-the-box new face from the youth team, they never forced me to get out of the back seat. In the end, one of the spaces there became a reserved seat for the 'VYP' (Very Young Player); that was me.

My longing to secure a Professional A contract was not the only reason why I was drawn closer to these players. While we (the C-contract players) had to clean our football boots by ourselves, A-contract players had Matsuura-san (Noriyoshi Matsuura), the first professional kit man in Japan, to take care of their boots. For them, a pair of muddy boots they left in their dressing room would always be waiting as a nice and shiny pair of boots on the following day. More important than avoiding having to clean your own boots, a professionally serviced pair of boots makes you feel more comfortable and less tired when wearing them.

To get to a place where I could have the 'magic hands' of Matsuura-san take care of my boots became one of my goals as a first-team player at Grampus. And the more I dwelt on that thick wall – both metaphorical and physical – separating us from the dressing room assigned to the A-contract players, the more strongly I felt, 'I don't want to be a C-contract player for long.'

A sea of red

The football god seemed to have been listening to my prayers and started answering them little by little, though it was in unfortunate circumstances for the team and some of the regular players that I got my big break. Following Marek Špilár, who picked up an injury on the opening day of the season, other centre-backs who were ahead of me in the pecking order began to join the former Slovakia international on the team's injury list. So came my first-team début. It was during the ninth league game of the season against Oita Trinita when I was told, 'Maya, you are on for the second half,' by the then manager, Sef Vergoossen.

I think I generally have a good memory, but when it comes to matches that I've been involved in, sometimes my memories remain exceptionally vivid. Maybe they are stored in a special drawer in my memory bank. I'm going to focus on key matches in my career in each chapter of this book, each one illustrating my 'samurai resilience'.

My choice for this chapter has to be a J.League game against Urawa Red Diamonds on 19 May 2007. It was the game in which I received my first proper harsh lesson as a professional player at Grampus, a narrow defeat (1–2) due to a late winner scored by the former Brazil international striker, Washington (full name: Washington Stecanela Cerqueira).

It was also my full début in front of our home crowd, though I had already been in the starting 11 in the previous two away games. As soon as I ran out for the pre-match warm-up, I was just amazed and went, 'Oh my God.' The packed stadium was a sea of red, as this was the main team colour for both Grampus and Urawa Reds.

Besides, I had never seen with my own eyes from the pitch the Toyota Stadium with almost 35,000 spectators packed inside it. The football stadium, the home ground of Grampus, was opened in July 2001. I had watched many games there since an intra-squad game opened the stadium, but the electric atmosphere on that day of the Urawa Reds game was something out of this world to me at the time.

And I was going to play in the starting line-up in that game. I felt an adrenaline rush just from being on the pitch in that atmosphere. I was still gazing at the packed stadium and trembling with excitement at the prospect of playing against one of the big guns in the J.League, when Toshiya-san ran up to me and said, 'Isn't this great, Maya?' I answered 'Yes!', but he'd already moved on.

'How cool is he?' I thought admiringly, as he made his way confidently about the pitch.

However, all I felt inside me right after the game was disappointment in defeat and frustration about my inability to prevent the winning goal, scored by the opposing team's lone striker. Washington, who spearheaded the Urawa Reds' attack, was a strong centre-forward and had been the J.League's top scorer in the previous season. At that time there weren't many players in the league who could stop this clinical 6' 2" finisher. So when the manager told me, 'Be prepared. You'll be starting,' the day before the game, I'd honestly thought, 'What? Really? Can I deal with Washington?'

On balance, though, my overall performance against Washington in that game wasn't too bad. To this day, I don't mind facing strikers like him, whose main attribute is physical strength.

A small margin but a big difference

There were only five or six minutes remaining in the second half. The moment I saw Washington receive the ball to his feet from the right, he turned the other way to shake off his marker and shot with his right foot. I was about a yard away from him, and tried to block his shot with my outstretched leg, but I could only make the slightest connection with the ball. To make matters worse, that tiny deflection changed the flight and took the ball away from the arm of our goalkeeper flying to make a save behind me.

'If I could have touched just a little bit more of the ball …' The fact that it shaved my leg made my frustration stronger; it was such a small margin between blocking a shot and conceding a goal. I told myself afterwards, 'I have to close that small gap which makes such a big difference. Otherwise, I can't make it to the top in the professional football world. This is the world where only those who make a difference by using that slight margin to their advantage can survive.' This thought was etched deeply in my mind on that day and has lived with me ever since.

Even now, I sometimes say, 'It's a matter of whether I can get one step or half a step closer,' after the game. I have been trying my hardest to close that gap, but as you make progress towards a higher standard there's always still a gap to close: a gap that makes a difference between winning and losing. And that difference can mean life or death in the world of professional football.

As a youth player I was almost invincible in aerial battles. I almost always came out as a winner. But against Washington I just about managed to make his life less comfortable when competing in the air. Not only the resulting defeat, but also the whole 90 minutes, was a really tough lesson for me on that day. The god of football certainly seems to be good at using a carrot-and-stick method to keep me motivated ...

Two former 'teachers'

Sef, the first manager I had as a professional footballer, was a very forgiving boss. It may be a common characteristic among managers and coaches from the Netherlands, his native country, but he was especially tolerant of positive mistakes by young players. Having said that, he must have needed great patience to keep playing me in my first year in the first team. Back then, I made two or three mislaid passes per game. There was one occasion when my mind was so preoccupied with making a forward pass to a team-mate's feet that I actually passed the ball instead to the opponent's striker standing right in front of me. But Sef still kept using me.

However, even he would surely have had second thoughts about playing me if the team had kept on conceding due to my mistakes. So I really have to thank Nara-san, our goalkeeper at that time. He kept making saves while this inexperienced centre-back kept making mistakes. Because of his skill in goal, my blunders didn't prove fatal to the team. Not only did he save us from conceding goals; he also saved me from being dropped to the bench on countless occasions – a true guardian of young Maya Yoshida.

In his managerial style, Sef seemed to me more of a teacher type than a typical football coach. He saw a player's behaviour both on and off the pitch as an important part of his quality as a professional. If a player did or said something deemed inappropriate by the manager, he wouldn't be playing afterwards, even if he was good enough to be a national team player. Sef had that sort of disciplinarian side to him, too.

In contrast, Dragan Stojković, aka Piksi, who succeeded Sef at Grampus in 2008, was a very demanding manager even to young players.

He was my idol in his playing days. When I was little, he was merely a player whom I liked, but after I joined the academy at Grampus, the club where he became a legend thanks to his brilliant technique and creative vision, I started to see Piksi as my hero. When he hung up his boots in 2001, I even went to watch his farewell ceremony at the stadium. So I was simply overjoyed to have an opportunity to play in a team managed by him.

He still had outstanding ball skills even several years after his retirement. On the training ground he could deliver an inch-perfect pass to a receiver's feet; sometimes he was angry with himself when he thought the quality of the pass was not up to his ultra-high standard.

He set the standards for his players quite high, too, and rightly so, never overlooking a single mistake in a game. The former *fantasista* known for his deft touches had a strict side as a manager. He may have been known for his good looks but his face was nothing but scary when he pointed out the mistakes we had made in a game and demanded an immediate response from us to improve. In one team meeting, while he was shouting at us, 'Why did you guys concede such a cheap goal?!' he banged a whiteboard he was using so hard that a magnet stuck to the board's surface came flying towards me.

As it turned out, having a forgiving and understanding manager, almost like a school teacher, in my first year as a professional, and then a much more demanding and strict manager in my second year, seemed to help me greatly in terms of my first-team survival. My ideal style of football – the skeleton of which took shape while I was coached by Mr Pak as a youth player – was fleshed out under Sef and Piksi, my first two managers as a professional footballer. I have added more substance to that skeleton ever since, and being someone who is good at learning from people around me I still keep on fleshing it out as a Premier League player, too.

From the motherland to the Netherlands

At the end of the year 2009, it was time for me to switch stages to perform as a footballer outside Japan. A new challenge began when I signed a three-and-a-half-year contract with VVV-Venlo in the Eredivisie, the first division in the Dutch football league.

If someone were to ask me whether it was an easy decision to leave Grampus, where I had spent nine years since joining its academy, my answer would be, 'No, it wasn't.' The people at Grampus, including managers, coaches and senior players, had taught me to grow both as a professional footballer and as a young man. It was there in Nagoya where the foundation of today's Maya Yoshida was formed.

But I believed that I was making the right decision in my professional career, and that it wouldn't be wrong to leave the club at that point. I even thought that a young Grampus player going abroad to advance his career would be beneficial to the club in the long term, so the Grampus supporters shouldn't be feeling too sad about me leaving the club.

How did my parents and brothers take my decision? Well, I don't really remember, to tell you the truth. I rarely ask my family members for advice and I certainly don't remember asking them, 'I want to move abroad to play, but what do you think?' before deciding to move to VVV. That now makes me wonder how they would have reacted had I made wrong decisions when I was younger. Would any member of the *laissez-faire* Yoshida family have told off their youngest boy? I'm not sure, but then again, I don't think I'd have made the sort of rash decisions some young people do.

Having said that, it was not like I had many options to consider before making a decision at that time. VVV were the only club I could go to if I wanted to move to Europe. I had just three years of experience in the J. League as a professional with no particular achievements even at the domestic level. There was no way for such a player to attract much interest from clubs abroad. On top of that, only a handful of Japanese were playing in Europe at the time and it was still difficult for a younger generation, my generation of Japanese players, to go abroad, even if we were keen to try.

For me, the move only became realistic six months or so after Honda-san's (Keisuke Honda) move to VVV. Other Japanese playing in Europe around that time were all from an older generation, such as Shunsuke Nakamura (then at Celtic) and Daisuke Matsui (then at Saint-Étienne). Under those circumstances, a young player like myself, the nobody of nobodies, had no right to complain about having no choice of foreign clubs to move to. I was just fortunate to share the same agent as Honda-san and was able to count on his strong connections with VVV.

It was the summer of 2008, the year of the Beijing Olympics. At the Shenyang Olympic Sports Center Stadium in China my agent was watching a men's Group B game between Japan and the Netherlands in the stadium with Mr Hai Berden, the chairman of VVV.

I'd only just made the Japan national Under-23 squad for Beijing and was not involved in the first two group games. But my chance finally came in our third game against the Netherlands, with Japan's elimination from the tournament already confirmed after two defeats.

We had nothing other than our pride to play for, but for the Netherlands a place in the knockout stage was still at stake. Therefore we faced a strong Dutch side and I was fortunate to have the chance to play against attacking talents such as Roy Makaay (then at Feyenoord) and Ryan Babel (then at Liverpool) while the chairman of VVV watched on from the stand. And it was right there that a conversation between Mr Berden and my agent took place – one that can be very simply summarised as follows:

Mr Berden: 'That defender looks quite good.'

My agent: 'He's our player.'

Mr Berden: 'Oh, well, we shall make an approach then.'

Since I already had a vision of furthering my career step by step overseas, I didn't have any problem at all with making my first step abroad in the Netherlands. In fact, I welcomed the challenge, as it was the country I could imagine myself moving to and playing football in based on past experience at least. Just before I became a high-school student in Japan I'd briefly had a chance to visit the Netherlands with a Grampus youth team, and had watched league games there and played against some local youth sides.

Some people were strongly against my decision to leave Grampus for VVV, saying, 'Why do you have to move to such a small club in the Netherlands?' But to me it was never that I felt I 'had to' move there, and it wasn't like I chose VVV instead of some bigger clubs in other countries.

Piksi, my manager at Grampus, was also against the move at that point in my career. 'It's too early for you,' he told me, on more than one occasion. Every time we spoke about my possible transfer, he said, 'It's not too late if you move after at least one more year here,' or, 'You'd better have enough under your belt before you move abroad,' as he tried to persuade me to stay.

A 500 per cent increase in earnings?

Talking about someone trying to persuade me to stay at Grampus, I have to mention Mr Kazumasa Kume, then the General Manager of the club. He used to call me to his office a few times a week and each time gave me a passionate talk. Listening to him, and looking at a line chart he drew on a whiteboard, it almost felt as though I were taking a lecture on 'Maya Yoshida's career plan'.

In the line chart, the vertical axis represented my annual salary, while the horizontal axis represented time until the 2010 World Cup. The first plot was drawn close to the crossing point of the two axes, meaning my salary at the time was low. Then he started with something like, 'Look, your current pay package is only around this level,' followed by, 'But we'll get Tulio next year.' Marcus Tulio Tanaka was a Brazil-born centre-back who was already one of the mainstays both at Urawa Reds and in the Japan national team at that time. Mr Kume continued talking, ignoring how shocked I was to hear that kind of 'top secret'. 'Playing with Tulio as a centre-back pairing must surely increase your chance of being called up to the national team,' he told me, and then he started drawing a positively sloped line. 'That can bring your next year's salary up around here. If you do get your first Japan call-up, we'd increase your bonus up to this level.

It even goes up to around here if you help us win the J.League title. Together with remunerations relating to national team appearances in the World Cup, your earnings can increase to this much,' explained Mr Kume, adding a much higher final plot than the first one in his chart.

For a little while, such 'lectures' continued in a similar vein every two or three days. And every time, I responded 'Yes' with a nod while he was talking, only to tell him, 'But I'll go to the Netherlands,' at the end. However hard he tried to persuade me to stay – whether by saying, 'I already have such a clear plan for you here,' or 'You'll be able to earn that much in a short time while you are only earning this much now' – my response was always, 'I understand, but I'm leaving for the Netherlands,' or 'Yes, but I'm still leaving.' In the end, he gave in and said, 'You're such a stubborn guy. If you are that determined, go!'

As a player, I was grateful for the club's assiduous efforts to persuade me to stay. I would be lying if I said that I didn't waver one bit. We are called professional footballers because we earn money by playing football. At that time my salary was around 20m yen (approx. £130,000) per year. People may say that such a figure is more than a decent amount for a 21-year-old, but the retirement age comes a few decades earlier for a footballer than for a corporate worker. You need to earn as much as you can in your playing career in order to be prepared for a long post-retirement life.

According to the plan Mr Kume had for me at Grampus, my annual earnings, including various bonuses, could eventually have reached around 100m yen (approx. £670,000). It was as if I was listening to someone explaining how I could earn five times more. The final amount he mentioned would have been twice as much as what I was supposed to earn if I eventually moved to VVV.

Part of me was thinking, 'Seriously? It's 100m yen we're talking about.' Even if I didn't get a call-up to the national team and was left with no appearances in the 2010 World Cup, his figures would still have meant a 400 per cent increase to my annual earnings at that time. I could have earned around 30m yen (approx. £200,000) more than the money I was being offered by VVV. Twenty-one-year-old Maya Yoshida thought twice, or thrice, about it.

However, although I felt a little temptation in terms of improving my financial situation, I was resolute enough in my determination to play abroad to enhance my career as a footballer. I said to Mr Kume, 'But if I say now that I'll stay for the pay rise, would you be really happy? Would you really like such a player? I don't think you would.' With that, I managed to convince the club that there could be only one outcome to our discussions, and that was me going abroad.

But there was one occasion on which I came close to having real second thoughts about leaving Grampus. It was at the last home game of the 2009 J.League season. After the final whistle, the players went out for the customary lap of appreciation. I remained on the bench in that game but still joined my team-mates to walk round the pitch and thank our supporters for their help throughout the season. Then a banner displayed in the stand behind one of the goals caught my eye.

It said, 'We're still in the middle of our journey. Let's continue together.' Something like that. A message from the Grampus supporters to me. It was still about a month before my transfer to VVV became official, but rumours had been going around for some time.

In my nine years at the club I had never seen a player receive a plea to stay from our supporters in such a manner. There is a kind of cool side to my personality, but I was touched when I saw that banner and felt the supporters' feelings towards me. In my mind I was moving steadily towards the Netherlands, but it felt like my stride was breaking a little. 'Am I right to leave here where people care about me this much?' I thought. That moment, on the day of the last home game of the season, was the only time I had something close to conflicted feelings in my mind, which, until then, had been resolved on a move to the Netherlands.

Baptism of fire

When they hear about a footballer's transfer to a European club, people might imagine that all their needs involved in the move are catered for. That may be true if you are moving to one of the biggest clubs in Europe, but more often a player is expected to cope with settling in by themselves. That is the first challenge a player faces, well before they actually start trying to perform on the pitch. From the start, you are likely to be in a situation that you never thought you would need to deal with.

I wasn't an exception to this scenario when I first moved to the Netherlands. At Grampus I was at a club where every aspect of my life as a player was taken care of. But at VVV it was different. I was now one of the non-EU players, to whom the club had to guarantee a certain level of wage to comply with league regulations – an outsider.

I imagined that various essentials for life in a foreign country – such as a house, maybe a car and a mobile phone – would be arranged for me by the club. But I was wrong. That is not how it works outside Japan. Everything like that is the individual's responsibility. If I said, 'Can you arrange this for me?' I would be told, 'Can you do it by yourself?' That was the reality. When I told the club that I would need a car, the reaction I got was, 'Oh, do you? Take the one that Keisuke used to drive, then. It's still here.'

I said, 'That'll do for now,' and got the key for the car Honda-san was using before his transfer to CSKA Moscow. It was an Audi A3. Once inside I had a quick look around, and found the rear seats were covered with dog hairs from his beloved *shiba inu*. It was more like an Audi K9 (canine). Honda-san, honestly!

He left for Moscow after the second year of a four-year car-lease contract, and for the club it would have been ideal if they could avoid paying the contract cancellation fee. There I was, a bit like a lamb to the slaughter, taking up the remaining two years of the lease contract. So, I had the car.

It was a challenge not to feel frustrated or irritated by the time it took to sort out some basic stuff involved in living in a foreign country. No doubt, those moving abroad to work or study experience much the same problems.

Of course, the real challenge as a footballer was waiting for me. It was much tougher than I expected, too.

I had a vision of making a steady adaptation to a new European league, but I ended up not being able to take a single step forward at the start of my time at VVV. Pain I had started to feel in my left ankle just before my transfer turned out to be caused by the metatarsal and I was diagnosed with a metatarsal stress fracture at a Dutch hospital upon my return from the team's training camp in Turkey. The injury required surgery. I even had to have a second operation several months after the original one.

By the time I was able to make my Eredivisie début, some ten months had passed since my transfer from Grampus at the end of the first half of the Dutch football season. I wasn't able to be on the pitch as a VVV player even once during the 2009/10 season.

I wouldn't blame the local supporters if they thought, 'Was he here?' On the other hand, they probably never forget the fact that Eredivisie clubs are obliged by the league regulations to pay foreign players a much higher salary than domestic players. At a small club like VVV, where the average annual salary of Dutch players would have been around 4m to 5m yen (£27,000 to £33,000), I, as a foreign player, must have been paid around ten times more than the domestic players during my time there. It was only natural if the fans thought, 'But he's not doing anything here,' about me in my first season at the club.

If there was any solace for me at that time, it was the fact that my listening comprehension in English, let alone in Dutch, was still limited, so abuse from the locals would have passed me by. If I had understood what was being said about me, and been criticised perhaps for earning a substantial wage for doing nothing, that might have dealt even a resilient mind such as mine a near-fatal blow, given that I was already feeling low during a long reha-bilitation after two operations.

Before the following 2010/11 season started, my squad number was changed from 28 to 3, as the defender who'd previously been wearing the No. 3 shirt had been released by the club. He was a popular and long-serving player, regarded as 'Mr VVV' by supporters. Before he left the club he had a dig at me: 'You're on a good salary even if you haven't played a single game, but don't worry about me. I just got released.' I knew he had a dry sense of humour but it still hurt. I was unable simply to laugh it off.

His cynical joke made me aware that a foreign player like myself joining the club could mean someone like him being pushed out of the squad at the same time. It was true that I ended up taking the place and shirt number of a local hero at VVV. It was also true that I actually hadn't done anything for the club so far at that point in my first year there. 'Shame on you, Maya. Out with injury as soon as you arrive here,' I said to myself. I was angry with myself for not being able to help my new team-mates on the pitch. But it also made me determined to perform to the best of my ability once the injury was behind me so that 'Mr VVV' would give me his approval as a worthy successor to the No. 3 shirt. That determination drove me on, even before I was physically able to take my first step forward as a footballer on foreign soil.

World citizen and Japanese

Moving abroad to the Netherlands was the first step in a process to internationalise myself. That is the way I see it. To me, having been to some foreign countries or being able to speak one or two foreign languages doesn't mean you are a true cosmopolitan. Once you feel comfortable in your own skin even in an alien environment, surrounded by different languages, cultures or customs from your own, and you become accepted as yourself in that environment, then you can call yourself a world citizen. Becoming one myself would be a very difficult goal to achieve.

Footballers go overseas for matches or training camps quite often, but going to a foreign country to live there is another matter. When you go abroad as a team member there is usually an interpreter and a coordinator accompanying the team to help you, and everything should go more or less smoothly as long as you follow the team schedule.

However, if you move overseas on your own, as a footballer does when transferred to a foreign club, nothing is done for you, let alone carefully planned, unless you take the initiative. You need constantly to make your own decisions.

This may be something that we Japanese are not particularly good at, because of our upbringing. At school, the prevailing ethos is mainly about collective behaviour; having a strong opinion of your own or standing out in some other way may not be appreciated. But when you start living abroad, you need to organise things for yourself: setting up a mobile phone contract with a local network, for example, unless you want to find yourself without a provider weeks after your arrival. Finding myself responsible for making numerous small but important decisions was the biggest shock I experienced when I first joined VVV. Nothing was as easy as I would expect in Japan.

Once you get used to the situation, and don't expect others to go the extra mile for you, you can adapt to the less pressurised European way. But, at first, as a Japanese, you can't help but find the slow pace inconvenient and feel it takes too long to get anything done in Europe.

In a small town in the Netherlands, it is not unusual to find that only a church and a few bakeries are open on Sunday. On top of that, even when shops are open on weekdays, you may not always find what you are looking for in stock and end up having to place an order, which, in turn, may take far too long to arrive from a Japanese point of view. If, by some misfortune, a member of the shop staff who dealt with your order is going to be away on holiday during its lead time, you might not even be able to chase your order for a little while.

When I first moved into a flat in Venlo, I didn't have curtains for my windows for more than two months. Had the flat been in Japan, the previous tenant might have left them there, but in the Netherlands, so I was told, there is a strict rule that the tenant must put the place back to its original state by stripping out anything added or replaced for personal use or taste, including wallpapers even, when vacating the property.

Again, in Japan, all you would need to do is measure the size of your windows, go to a DIY home centre and buy ready-made curtains. However, in the Netherlands curtains are usually made to order. As my arrival in the flat coincided with a local carnival, which meant all the townspeople – including the shop-owners – were celebrating for days on end, I didn't even hear from the shop about the delivery date of my curtains for almost a month after I placed the order.

For other Japanese people, the order may have taken even longer to arrive than it did in my case. I don't mean that I received special treatment because of my occupation. It's just that Japanese people are sometimes disrespected, as we tend to look much younger than our age to Western people. In this regard, I'm an exception. More often than not, people tell me I look older than I am; I was repeatedly teased about this when I was young. But in Europe it is more of an advantage. I shall proudly call it the strength of an 'old bloke's face'.

As well as the slow customer service, another issue I struggled with in the Netherlands was the food. It is safe to say that Japan has developed a very rich and varied food culture. Dutch people, though, don't seem to mind having almost the same menu day after day. At least, it seemed that way to me when I was living in Venlo. They would eat some bread with ham and cheese for breakfast, and for lunch too. Small variations could be fried eggs or a pot of yoghurt. I thought that sort of diet was questionable in terms of sports nutrition, and simply as a Japanese, never mind a footballer, I found the diet in the Netherlands quite tough to get used to.

As a typical Japanese, I would like to have some rice at least once a day. That meant cooking my own evening meals in Venlo. Having left my home town in my early teens, I don't really mind cooking for myself, but that doesn't mean I'm a good cook. My cooking repertoire is limited, and it became even more limited in Europe. If I wanted to cook one of my standard recipes called *Buta Kimchi* (pork and kimchi stir fry), for example, it would be difficult to find some thinly sliced pork and kimchi (a Korean staple with spicy fermented cabbage) in a local supermarket.

That was one of the reasons why I often spent my dinner time with a fellow Japanese footballer, 'Uchiy' (Atsuto Uchida), who was a full-back at FC Schalke 04 when I was at VVV. Venlo is situated in the south-eastern part of the Netherlands and is close to the German border. So I used to drive into Germany to join him for a meal prepared by a housekeeper at his place or to eat out with him at a Japanese restaurant in Düsseldorf, a half-way point from each other's place. Fortunately, Düsseldorf has the second-largest Japanese community in Europe after London, so I could also buy what I needed to cook *Buta Kimchi* when I went there to dine with Uchiy, which was as often as twice a week.

For someone living in Japan, both the Netherlands and Germany are faraway foreign countries, but once you're in Europe you can travel back and forth between these two adjoining nations very easily. Without the need to show a passport at the border, it is much like driving to a neighbouring prefecture in Japan.

Making a frequent car journey between two European countries just to eat dinner may sound very international and cosmopolitan. But there are responsibilities that come with being a foreigner abroad, especially when you are part of a small community from a particular country.

As Venlo is such a small town, I was a public figure of sorts in the local society, as a foreign player who had come to the local club. It didn't matter that I was an obscure figure before the transfer. My relatively high profile in such a small place made me aware that I could harm the reputation of other Japanese living in the town. If, for instance, I behaved badly, such as driving selfishly, having a row on a night out or being rude to locals, people in Venlo might say, 'What's wrong with the Japanese?' rather than questioning Maya Yoshida individually. Something I might do could result in all Japanese people there being viewed in the same negative way.

Whichever country or city I go to, there is always a chance that there are some Japanese people who have been living there before my arrival. If so, they will have been there working, raising a family and being accepted as respected residents. The one thing I would never want to do, as a new Japanese on the block, is to damage the reputation of other Japanese in an area. This was especially the case in a small place like Venlo where, I imagined, it might be difficult as a foreigner to gain acceptance into local society. I became extremely conscious after I moved to the Netherlands that I must not do anything to make the life of other Japanese residents difficult.

No risk, no future

For the first six months or so at VVV, there were hardly any other Japanese players nearby whom I could go to see in my free time. It was different, though, when I returned to Venlo after the second operation on my left foot and subsequent rehabilitation in Japan. I didn't even have to drive to see Robert Cullen (a half-Japanese), as he became my team-mate at VVV. Michihiro Yasuda also came to the Netherlands to play for SBV Vitesse. In the meantime, Shinji Kagawa at Borussia Dortmund, Tomoaki Makino and Jong Tae Se (a Nagoya-born Korean) at 1.FC Köln, Hajime Hosogai at FC Augsburg and Takashi Inui at VfL Bochum joined Uchiy in Germany.

The Ruhr region was a major industrial region, now suddenly it became an 'industrial area' producing Japanese Bundesliga players. We all used to get together in Düsseldorf, which was only about a 30-minute drive away for every one of us.

Although I spent a lot of time in Düsseldorf, I wouldn't hesitate to recommend the Netherlands as a starting point if I was asked for advice by younger Japanese players who want to play in Europe. I wonder sometimes why there aren't more Japanese coming to play in the Dutch league now.

So many top-class footballers have come from the Netherlands, such as the legendary Johan Cruyff, whose death in March 2016 was mourned internationally. For such a small country – its land area is roughly the same as the island of Kyushu, where I was from – it has exported an incredible number of players to major European leagues, including the Spanish La Liga, Italian Serie A, German Bundesliga and the Premier League.

The Netherlands is one of the most advanced football nations in the world, with its national team having been finalists in three World Cups and the winners of Euro 1988. They failed to qualify for the 2018 World Cup in Russia, but the fact that their failure to reach the finals in Russia was big news proves that they have been one of the major football forces in the world over many years. The Netherlands made it to the last four in the previous World Cup in Brazil, and there were still more than 20 Dutch players in the Premier League in the 2017/18 season.

Needless to say, it is an advanced country as a nation, too. And in terms of the language, the Netherlands is one of the most English-friendly countries in the world among those where English is not the first language. It is initially puzzling, then, that there aren't more Japanese footballers.

My explanation for this is as follows.

Currently, there is no foreign player quota in the Eredivisie, the first division of the Dutch league. To sign someone from abroad, its clubs, in order to conform with league regulations, must guarantee a certain level of salary. The minimum salary for such players is set at one and a half times higher than the average salary of Dutch players registered in the league. During the time I was at VVV, an annual salary of somewhere around 40m to 50m yen (£270,000 to £330,000) was commonly offered to a foreign player.

For a J.League player, one would have to reach a certain level to earn a salary in that region. But it also means that such a player, even a young one around 20 years of age, might well be offered a chance to play in Europe by a Dutch club with a salary in the similar region. If so, that player might be tempted by a move to that club.

But at the same time, the J.League club to whom the player is under contract would almost certainly try to make him stay by offering an improved salary when it came to opening talks over a new contract. Then the player in question would have to make a choice. That could be, let's say, whether to move to a Dutch club offering a 50m yen (£330,000) annual salary, or to stay at the J.League club on an improved contract of 70m yen (£470,000) annual salary. I believe it is not uncommon for a J.League player to choose the latter, as it also involves less risk on and off the pitch.

Then what happens if the same player renews his interest in playing abroad in his mid- to late twenties? I have to say that if he is a Japanese defender in his late twenties with very limited English but still wanting to play in Europe, the best he could wish for would be an offer from a second division club in a country such as Belgium or the Netherlands. And I think he would need to be prepared to take a less attractive offer; a three-year contract with a 20m yen (approx. £134,000) per year salary, for instance.

Does he still want to go abroad? Many would hesitate, I guess, especially if the player is already earning around three times more as a J.League player. I wouldn't be surprised if quite a few Japanese players lose their chance to play abroad by failing to make a decision to do so at the right moment.

In short, playing abroad represents a bit of a risk, compared to the more secure and financially lucrative option of staying in Japan. I had to make that choice when Mr Kume drew that line chart in front of me at Grampus. However, when you take the risk, there is also the chance of receiving a bigger reward in the future – with hard work and a bit of luck, you may be able to reach a much higher level as a footballer as well as an earner.

As a J.League player, no matter how good you are, the maximum amount you can earn at a club is set at around 150m yen (approx. £1m) per year according to the league's contractual regulations. On the other hand, in Europe the vertical axis representing a player's salary can extend without limit for as long as your value as a player is recognised by your club. As a professional player, it is possible to get yourself a pay package of 400m yen (approx. £2.7m) or even 500m yen (approx. £3.3m) per year, which you could never get as a Japanese playing in the J.League. If you're willing to make a brave decision at an early juncture in your career, not as a gamble but as part of the vision you have for your own future as a professional player, it can make a huge difference to your future prospects.

Sometimes, a young Japanese player will say to me, 'You must be comfortably off, Maya-san.' When that happens, I feel like answering, 'It's because I'd made decisions to realise my vision for my future ever since I was a teenager. Have you done the same? Can you make such a decision?' I even say exactly that sometimes, depending on whom I'm talking to.

Unless you are prepared to make decisions and act to realise your vision, you are likely to end up wasting your opportunity. So long as it is not too late for them yet, then, I always tell people, 'If you want to, you should go now. Otherwise, it will be very difficult to try playing abroad.'

The future I envisaged for myself as a professional player went beyond playing for VVV. So, when I began my second year there during the 2011/12 season I was already thinking, 'If I continue to play in this environment, I might struggle to reach another level.' Part of me, even then, was feeling a bit too comfortable with the culture at VVV, where mistakes made by young players were tolerated. I knew I would need to be in a harsher environment, where a single mistake could prove costly, in order to improve further as a player. It also seemed to be the right time to make my next step forward in Europe, as I was approaching my mid-twenties. I'd originally expected to move next to a more established Dutch club before I finally realised my dream of joining a Premier League outfit, but things were to take a surprising turn.

Offer from the Saints

Again, the god of football seemed to be smiling down on me. It all started after I was selected as one of the over-age players in the Japan national Under-23 squad for the 2012 London Olympics. Normally, a Japanese centre-back playing for VVV wouldn't be watched daily by scouts from British clubs, but with football matches for the tournament being held all over Britain, dozens of scouts were at the games.

The first game for Japan in Group D was against Spain (1–0) in Glasgow, which was followed by another win with the same scoreline against Morocco in Newcastle, then by a draw (0–0) against Honduras in Coventry. Once in the knockout stage, we beat Egypt (3–0) at Old Trafford in Manchester and made it to the semi-finals at Wembley Stadium (losing 3–1 to Mexico).

Obviously, scouts from local clubs and other British clubs were watching the young talents on show at each venue. After the game in Glasgow, I heard from my agent that Celtic, where Shunsuke Nakamura had been playing until 2009, were interested in me. After the game at St James' Park, it was Newcastle who showed an interest, according to my agent. There were also hints or rumours about other British clubs showing an interest in me. The fact that we, as a team, were in good form and making progress in the tournament helped me to attract more attention from various clubs.

Among those, Southampton was one of the first to show an interest in me and the only one to remain at the end. Other clubs might have come and gone but Southampton kept pursuing me. What they initially told me they could offer sounded very good to me, too. But they wanted to watch me play at least one league game at club level first, so the final decision on my future was postponed until the beginning of the following season.

When the time for the game on which rode my transfer to Southampton arrived, I had to play with almost no preparation. Following the Olympic Games, I had to join the Japan senior national team for an international friendly, which prevented me from taking part in VVV's pre-season training. On top of that, at VVV it was nothing unusual to see more than ten players replaced during the summer, as many players were there on loan due to the club's limited transfer budget.

As a consequence, in the third league game of the 2012/13 season, my first start in the new campaign at VVV, though I was playing to secure both three points and a ticket to Southampton, it felt like I was playing in a team in which I had never played before.

Result? We lost to Den Haag with four goals conceded.

Nonetheless, an official offer came from the other side of the North Sea the day after what I could call the most important game of my professional life so far. The goddess of victory may have turned her back on us in what turned out to be my last game as a VVV player, but the Saints didn't abandon me (though the salary offered in the end was much lower than I'd initially been told!).

The fact that I could join Southampton was much more important than how much I would earn by joining them. My mind was made up to go for the transfer. Because I was already in the last year of my contract, VVV too were quite keen to make it happen while they could still sell me for a transfer fee, which they could then spend to bring a new player in. Things started moving quickly towards a conclusion and I signed a three-year contract with Southampton on 30 August 2012, in what I would describe as a 'win-win-win' situation for the seller (VVV), the buyer (Southampton) and the player (myself).

For someone who had long dreamed of being a Premier League player, I had almost no idea about Southampton before the transfer started to happen. Just about the only thing I knew about the club was that Chung-kun (nickname of Tadanari Lee, from his Korean name Chung-Sung Lee) had joined it earlier in the same year.

Of course, I asked him about the club during our phone conversations and his answers were always positive. As I was so keen on the move from the start, my first impressions about Southampton got better and better. I did have a shade of anxiety in my mind, though, to be honest. My sole source of information about the club, Chung-kun, had only been there for six months or so, and it was his first club outside Japan. I wondered a little if it was wise to accept whatever he was telling me about the club without question.

However, it was nothing new for me to apparently have little choice when it came to making an important decision. I was at an important juncture in my football life, just as I had been when I moved to Nagoya as a 12-year-old, and when I left Grampus to join VVV at 21.

So, after two and a half years in the Netherlands, this samurai of a footballer was now ready to move on to the south coast of England for a new battle, by answering the call from the Saints.

CHAPTER 3

MOTHERLAND OF FOOTBALL

Baptism of fire in a humbling début

On 15 September 2012, at the Emirates Stadium in north London, the Premier League début I had dreamed about since my teenage years suddenly became a reality at the home of Arsenal – one of the English giants.

For Southampton, it was the fourth league game in the 2012/13 season, and the fifth in all competitions since the opening day. But for me, whose transfer from VVV-Venlo had only been finalised officially on 30 August, it was the very first time I was named in a match-day squad as a Southampton player. So, when my début came in the 28th minute of the first half, it was actually a real surprise for me.

I must have looked completely disconcerted, and I certainly felt it. In less than 10 minutes after I came on the pitch, Arsenal's lead was extended from one to four goals. It felt as though I had been pushed off a cliff.

On that day, I don't think I was prepared to stand on even a cliff edge. After the game, Nigel Adkins, then the manager of Southampton, said at the post-match press conference that I'd only had two days to train with the team at my new club. He wasn't simply protecting his new centre-back. It was the truth. And even those two training days weren't what could be described as real team sessions. I'd been quite happy on the morning of the Arsenal game when the manager told me, 'Just soak up the atmosphere of a Premier League game from the bench. That's all you need to do today.'

I was in the squad and arrived at the stadium on the team coach, but inside I was feeling like a 'tourist'. From the moment the magnificent 60,000-seater stadium came into sight through the coach window, I kept saying, 'Wow!', dazzled by everything I saw or felt. Once we were inside the stadium and went to check out the pitch, I was thinking, 'Wow. It looks like a huge green carpet.' As I stepped onto it, I went 'Wow!' again. The pitch looked and felt like a high-quality carpet, ideal for the home team, who were known for their pass-and-move style of football. I spotted one of the Arsenal players, and couldn't hide my excitement. 'There goes Walcott!' I said to myself.

I was still in that distracted frame of mind on the bench when the manager suddenly asked me, 'Maya, can you play?' around halfway through the first 45 minutes. One of our centre-backs, Jos Hooiveld, got injured, and the only centre-back among our substitutes was me, who was supposed to be a 'spectator on the bench' for that game.

If you are a footballer, and playing in the Premier League has been your dream, there is no way you will answer, 'I can't, because I'm not ready,' to your manager when he asks if you can come on. No one will do that. Never. I certainly didn't. I said, 'Yeah, I can!' straight away.

In reality, I was so not ready that I couldn't even remember many of my team-mates' names. The only ones I could recall once I was on the pitch were José Fonte, the other centre-back who had started the game with Jos, and Foxy (Danny Fox), who was playing as a left-back. As I couldn't remember the name of the central midfielder (Morgan Schneiderlin) playing in front of me, I had to ask after I came on. I was like, 'What's his name? What? Morgan? Got it. Morgan, it is.' It was almost impossible not to feel nervous, in such circumstances.

Just seven minutes after replacing the injured Jos, I received my first brutal lesson as a novice Premier League player when I let Gervinho run on to a long ball into the space behind and score in a one-on-one with our goalkeeper. I'd thought I had Gervinho under control. But when I saw the ball from midfield going over my head and turned to look behind, the back of the Arsenal striker was already about two yards ahead of me. In my first game as a Southampton defender, my mistake led directly to a goal conceded.

I just can't switch off even for a second, I told myself. If I do, I will get punished.

That first lesson in the Premier League was harsh indeed but it was worth learning, especially as it came so soon after my move to Southampton.

Over the course of the previous two months I had played in the London Olympics, followed it up with three games in Japan with the senior national side, and then played an Eredivisie game in the Netherlands, which was, in effect, my final audition to become a Southampton player. It really was an eventful summer. Coming to the Premier League in that incredibly busy summer of 2012 after putting in a lot of travel miles, my feet might not have been firmly on the ground when I finally fulfilled my dream and made my Premier League début. If it was a dream, then Arsenal soon woke me up and slapped me in the face, with three goals coming in quick succession before half-time.

In the second half, I was more like my normal self on the pitch, thinking, 'If I keep a cool head, I can make passes into a space here and there.' I wasn't going to go into my shell, despite what had happened in the first half soon after my introduction. I actually did feed the ball to our midfielders, initiated an attack or two by linking up with Morgan, whose name I had just relearned, sent a long ball to the front line, and even went up the pitch with the ball at my feet. With a big lead, the Arsenal players stepped off the gas a little, and that may have contributed to my improved second-half performance. Also, they were not a team known for hard pressing, although I wasn't fully aware of that on the day.

If the situation in which Gervinho scored his first goal in the game had happened not seven minutes after I came on, but seven minutes after the interval, I might have prevented him from running away to score. In the second half, with my composure regained, I was feeling quite positive, thinking, 'This really is where I want to be, in a real tough world at the top level.'

The game finished 6–1 to Arsenal, but though it was a baptism of fire I would still say that it has to be the key match in the first year of Maya Yoshida at Southampton. It was a heavy defeat on my début, but I didn't have a nightmare on the pitch that day. I just got a glimpse of the reality of the world that is the Premier League – a world that I had for so long yearned to be a part of.

Baptism of property agency

After my transfer from VVV, I needed a little bit of time to regain my composure off the pitch, as well as on it. As was the case when I moved to the Netherlands, there were challenges I had to face in order to start my life in a different country. It was very much all down to me in England as well.

Nowadays, in addition to finding a place to live, having a mobile phone and internet access could also be considered essentials that a player would want to sort out as quickly as possible after moving to a club in a foreign country. Ideally, he would also want to have a car to commute to and from the club's training ground. Once again, I had to arrange all of these things by myself after joining Southampton.

As an organisation, a Premier League club is much bigger than a small Eredivisie club, of course. But Southampton at that time had just been promoted from the Championship (second division) at the end of the previous season after seven years' absence from the Premier League, two of which were spent in League One (third division). The club is now in the hands of Chinese and Swiss owners, but had been in administration only about three and a half years before I joined.

Southampton has traditionally been a selling club; selling players developed through the club's youth scheme is part of its financial management. Gareth Bale, who later would move from Tottenham to Real Madrid in Spain after being voted the Player of the Year in the

2012/13 Premier League season, was one of the youth products at Southampton. When I joined, the place had a kind of homely domestic feel to it, as opposed to the global image which the Premier League projects around the world. True, there were other players from overseas apart from myself, but the majority of my team-mates were British.

Back then, Southampton didn't have a players' liaison officer. A liaison officer is a member of the club staff whom players can turn to for assistance for various reasons – for instance, when a foreign player receives a parking ticket but doesn't know how to pay the penalty charge. It's an important role at a club of any standing, but the position didn't exist at Southampton when I joined them.

Instead, it was one of my team-mates, Jos Hooiveld, who helped me to settle down quickly. It was he who accompanied me to a local shop to get a mobile phone contract sorted out. He's a genuinely nice guy, a top man, even among Dutch people who, it seems to me, are all kind-hearted. To him, I represented new competition in the team as a centre-back as well as a new team-mate, but he was still happy to help, even though he was only in his second year at Southampton and a bit of a newbie himself. He also helped me set up an internet connection at my place and arranged a car for me. If I joined the club now, everything would have been taken care of by the club's capable liaison officer, but at the time I was grateful for Jos's help.

Having said that, after going through my second transfer abroad, I now think I should try to do everything by myself as much as I can. That has become my attitude towards living in a foreign country. I now try to do everything myself first, and only when I find something too difficult or complicated do I ask for help from the liaison officer.

One day, when it is time for me to hang up my boots, I may still want to continue my life abroad. If so, there will be no liaison officer around to help a former player in his post-retirement life in a foreign country. If I stay in England and get some kind of job at Southampton, the club's liaison officer might extend a helping hand to one of its ex-players. But I wouldn't want to bother them, as the officer's job is to help current players at the club, not retired ones.

Besides, I didn't find things too problematic when I moved to England, thanks to my previous experience in the Netherlands. Over here everything is in English, too, so I wouldn't be completely at a loss when it comes to documents or notices.

All the same, I was rather shocked by one experience when I was trying to get the basics of my England life sorted. The problem arose when I was trying to find a place to live.

In Japan, when people hear the phrase 'property agency', they might picture a small, independent agency near a local station, which has been there for ages. At a good old-fashioned Japanese property agency they are happy for you to pop in without an appointment and to show you some properties after listening to what you are looking for. But over here, I felt like I, the potential customer, had to accommodate their schedule and priorities first. Sometimes they wouldn't even deal with me properly, saying, 'We're too busy at the moment,' and would hand me a business card as a cue for me to leave their office.

Their priority seemed to lie very much with customers interested in a property for sale, rather than for letting. I had heard that England had seen a housing bubble for over 10 years at the time. In this country, the value of a property is not only about its land price, unlike in Japan, where there is always a risk of earthquakes, and where house rebuilding is a common practice. In England, once you get the location right, the property value can increase as the years go by; thus many people are looking for a property to buy as an investment.

Also compared to Japan, where people tend to view buying a house as a lifetime financial commitment, it seems easier here to take out a mortgage. In England, it is not unusual for people to buy a property with a mortgage, then to take out another mortgage for another property by using the first property as security. No wonder, then, that property agencies are so busy with sales opportunities, given that they have a direct impact on staff bonuses.

What I was looking for when I moved from the Netherlands was a modern flat to rent in Southampton's redeveloped bay area. I could imagine many people were also looking for similar properties, but to buy to invest.

As I was clearly viewed as a low-priority customer, one of my early viewing appointments was almost meaningless. A property agent put in charge of my search not only forgot about the appointment and showed up late after receiving a call from me, but also didn't have a key to the property we were going to see and then realised it was already rented out. Staring at her aghast as she left with a cheery 'See you next time', I wanted to scream, 'I didn't really have "this time"! When the f*** is the next time!'

I'm known for my gentle nature (I think) but that experience made me furious. The estate agent was so unprofessional, forgetting the appointment to start with and then the keys. It was an appointment made to suit her 'busy' schedule, not mine.

As people over here tend to be more assertive than people in Japan in general, you also need to assert yourself sometimes. Otherwise, you might end up being treated like a pushover. That is one of the lessons of life I learned in the Netherlands. So I went to the property agency to complain.

But I couldn't simply lose my temper there. That is a no-no, especially for someone who wants to be a world citizen. Regardless of the fact that my English was not good enough to rant and rave at them, the most effective way to make a complaint and have it heard is to do it calmly and in a way that hits the spot where it hurts the most. I think that is universally true. So I said at the agency, 'I'm going to another property agency,' to let them know that I was pissed off by the way I was being dealt with.

Then they took me more seriously. I also said (I think), 'I'll never go for one of your properties.' But, in the end, the flat where I first lived as a Southampton player was found through that same property agency. It was the only property I liked among those I saw. Needs must. That is also universally true ...

Crowd with a high football IQ

Having begun my Premier League life on the pitch in week four of the 2012/13 season, I started in 31 of the remaining 34 league fixtures. My first start was at Villa

Park the following week, where we recorded our first league win after four defeats in a row from the opening day of the season. As one of the three promoted sides, Southampton were regarded as relegation candidates, but I learned much later, when we started picking up points, that some of our supporters were saying, 'Maya could be a saviour for us.' (My mind was so preoccupied with football that I hardly noticed their favourable views at that time.)

I considered the Saints supporters to be a warm-hearted bunch from day one. The fan base may be on a smaller scale compared to that of big clubs in the capital such as Arsenal, Tottenham or Chelsea, but the passion of our local supporters is certainly not any less. If anything, their support out on the pitch can sometimes feel even more intense.

For instance, I didn't find the atmosphere created by the big crowd at the Emirates Stadium, where I made my début, particularly intimidating. I remember thinking as I watched the game from the bench, 'The home supporters here seem quite gentle.'

Saints supporters, on the other hand, are always in good voice, whether at St Mary's Stadium, our home, or at an away ground. When they burst into a rousing rendition of 'When the Saints Go Marching In' at home, the atmosphere of the place is just like I dreamed it would be while watching Premier League games on DVD as a youth player in Japan. Feeling the passion and power of our supporters on the pitch galvanises me every time I hear them chanting.

Throughout my football career I have been blessed with loyal supporters. I felt very grateful for the supporters at Nagoya Grampus Eight where I came through the youth system, and at VVV where I had my first taste of playing in Europe, and I'm certainly feeling the same at Southampton where I'm now spending my sixth year since my move.

Some of the Japanese readers of this book might have a scary image of European football supporters, as if they are still the 'hooligans' from a few decades ago. It's true that you may still spot someone with a shaven head or a tattoo at a stadium, but the supporters I've encountered during my VVV days and now at Southampton are, in the vast majority of cases, passionate but not violent.

Of course, they can't always be merry. Saints supporters, too, can be critical of us at times. At VVV there were occasions when the home crowd continued to applaud a player if he was playing well, even if the team was losing the game 3–0. But I put that sort of reaction down to the unbelievably generous nature of VVV supporters. In Europe, in general, it is the norm for the crowd to let their frustration show if they find their team's performance or result not good enough.

Another difference between the home crowds at VVV and Southampton is their size. At VVV, attendance was around 8,000 people at the most, including those in standing sections, while St Mary's Stadium is a 32,000 all-seater. I can only feel privileged as a Southampton player to have four times more supporters behind the team when we fight for victory at home.

Supporters in England are also well known, universally I think, for their enthusiasm and ability to chant – even if they are sometimes ruthless with the barbs they aim at the opposition. I haven't experienced the South Coast derby against Portsmouth yet, as we have not been in the same division since I joined Southampton, but I know how fierce the chanting battle in the stands can be in England when it comes to local derbies.

I feel honoured when I hear the Saints supporters singing my name in a chant, such as 'Oh, Maya Yoshida!', during a game. By the way, is it a defender thing that chants for us back-line players don't seem to have the cool punchy words typical of those for attacking players? For instance, a chant for Nathan Redmond, our winger, cleverly rhymed 'lightning' and 'frightening'. Maybe I need to encourage the fans by exhibiting in the Premier League my secret weapon, a jumping volley, which earned me the accolade of best goal of the season from the Dutch media when I was playing for VVV. Wait till you see it with your own eyes, you Saints supporters!

Joking aside, the eyes of English supporters are as keen as their tongues. I have been very impressed by the crowds in the mother country of football. It seems to me that people here have a very high football IQ regardless of their age or gender. They react to subtle touches or interceptions by a defender with applause or audible gasps. I really love that sort of reaction from the stands. The match-day fans in Japan, too, are as passionate about the clubs they support as people in England, but that keen eye of the supporters here is certainly one of the pleasures I feel as a player in the Premier League.

In England, where many people support a certain club generation after generation, there are many families with kids at a game. Those kids can educate themselves about football by watching how people around them react to what is happening on the pitch. Their football eye can develop to spot a piece of good play, even if it's not as obvious as a superb shot or a well-timed last-minute tackle. I think that's part of the reason why countries like England produce top-quality players. People here start understanding what good play really is when they are very young simply by watching football, and their understanding increases every time they go and watch a game.

This means that by the time they actually start playing football themselves they already have a built-in memory containing a lot of knowledge of how to be a good player, which enables them to at least try to apply that understanding in their own play. That's how I think it works.

Japanese supporters, both old and young, tend to react with anticipation only when a well-known or popular attacking player has possession of the ball. The media over there also tend to emphasise such moments, because the entertainment value is higher for the TV audience. That may need to change if we sincerely care about the development of Japanese football, no matter how long it takes.

'Visitor team' or away team

I now live in a house with my wife and baby daughter in Winchester, whose population, around 45,000, is about the same as Nagasaki in Japan where I was born. It is a popular choice of residence among Southampton players. We sometimes share a car to Staplewood, where our training centre is located.

A little while ago, my wife and I had a small house party to celebrate our daughter's birthday with our friends – two Japanese women and their English husbands. While we were chatting, the two men started talking about Wayne Rooney. It was shortly after his drink-driving incident was in the news. One of the English men said he couldn't rate Rooney too highly because he had been in the spotlight for the wrong reasons off the pitch. The other argued, saying that we should judge him as a professional footballer based on what he could do and had done on the pitch, and praised his hugely successful career at the top level since he came on to the scene as a teenage phenomenon. They continued talking about his abilities, contributions to his teams and English football, and games in the past where Rooney's genius was on show. I was joining in here and there as I listened to their conversation, thinking, 'Dads engaging in a conversation about a football player at a kid's birthday party. This probably wouldn't happen in Japan.'

There might be a similar scene in Japan if the conversation was about baseball, the most popular professional sport in the country. I can easily see middle-aged Japanese men talking enthusiastically about a player, saying something like, 'He should've thrown a curveball instead of a screwball to that hitter.' But I think the same still cannot be said about football in Japan as a general topic in our casual conversations. Football in Japan is still in its developing stage in terms of its general popularity among the nation. It will take decades or even a century for football to be a part of people's everyday life, as it is in England.

People's fondness of and knowledge about football in England means they can sometimes be harsh critics as well as keen-eyed supporters. To play in this country, you need to get used to shouts such as 'Can't you even do that?' or 'Take him off!' from your own supporters. I don't think I've ever heard a chorus of 'You're not fit to wear the shirt!' at a J.League game.

English people at a football stadium are a far cry from the image of a traditional English gentleman we Japanese have in our mind. The same can be said about English ladies at a game. You can hear a female voice (not necessarily a shrill voice, as we would expect in Japan) screaming, 'What were you thinking?' or 'Wake up!' at a player who just mislaid a pass or made some other error.

When fans decide to boo or taunt an opposition player, the noise can get even louder. At a Premier League game, even if it's your home game, there can be away supporters in their thousands, and if it's an away game, you are surrounded by the opposition's 'twelfth player' in their tens of thousands. If you are on the receiving end of their abuse, it is an awful experience without a doubt.

At an away game, you really feel you are in the opposition's territory even before the game starts. In Japan, a team playing a game away from home is referred to as a 'visitor team', which, I think, has a feel of a welcomed guest to it. But here in England, if you are an away team, you'll be treated exactly like that. Your opponents have no intention of making you feel comfortable in their home. As far as the dressing room goes, there seems to be a general consensus here to make your opponent feel as uncomfortable as possible. For starters, the away dressing room is usually much smaller than the home dressing room. I couldn't believe my eyes when I saw the tiny away dressing room at Loftus Road, the home of Queens Park Rangers. Crystal Palace's Selhurst Park has a very small away dressing room, too.

On the other hand, when I went to the Emirates Stadium for what turned out to be my Premier League début game against Arsenal, feeling very much like a 'visitor' on the day, I said to myself, 'Wow, look how big it is!' when I stepped inside the away dressing room there. But it didn't take that long to realise that the Emirates Stadium was an exception. One of the away dressing rooms that I'm not really keen to be inside is at Everton's Goodison Park. I appreciate it's one of the oldest football stadiums in the world and has a very traditional English stadium feel, but the dressing room for the away team there is also very 'English', a space that is not supposed to provide comfort to its users. True to its 'minimalistic' design, it doesn't even have a wall separating the changing area and shower area, although the floor in the latter is lower to prevent water running into the changing area. Even so, once players start taking showers after the game, the room quickly becomes like a 'steam room', as if that is Everton's way of telling the opposing team that they are not welcome to stay.

When I have visited Old Trafford, I feel there are certain disadvantages for both teams. For a stadium called 'The Theatre of Dreams' the condition of the pitch is quite often not as beautiful as its nickname suggests, especially in the second half of the season. Also, the pitch slopes behind the corner flags, which I find not at all helpful for a corner-kick taker. Thinking about that, I just have to admire David Beckham even more for all the dangerous corner kicks he produced at home games as a Manchester United player.

Streetwise

At away games in England, I feel sometimes that referees' decisions tend to favour the home team, especially when it is a big club. Through such experiences I have learned the need to apply pressure onto the referee sometimes.

In Europe, especially in England, I hear the word 'streetwise' quite often when people talk about football. Many people, apparently, think that part of the reason why England have struggled at international tournaments is that their national team players are too honest; raised to play in a spirit of fair play, they are not crafty enough to solicit a favourable decision from the referee, which could make the difference between winning and losing in a tight game at international level.

I believe being streetwise on the pitch is something we Japanese are also not good at, both as individual players and as a team. In a big game, or a game at major international tournaments such as the World Cup, referees can get more cautious about the decisions they make. They may even hesitate when they need to make a big call, because they are only human. Under such circumstances they might be influenced unknowingly by constant pressure from players to give them a decision they want. But Japanese players seldom try to put pressure on a referee. Such reticence can be viewed as very sporting, but also as being overly meek.

For instance, when we play a World Cup qualifier against a Middle Eastern country, their players will constantly protest against the referee's decisions. They just keep at it. And over the course of 90 minutes the referee's decision often seems to start leaning towards them – what we call a 'whistle in the Middle East'. But even then, there aren't many Japanese players who try to do the same in order to get more balanced decisions. I think it is mainly because, in our culture, not complaining is seen as a virtue.

The spirit of fair play could be understood as a modern-day interpretation of the sense of justice underlining the old samurai spirit. In the world of the samurai, there was simply no place for cowards to live. But being streetwise and being cowardly are two different things. It may be that we need to consider pressuring a referee not as poor conduct but as part of a strategy to get a small advantage in order to secure a result in a game.

In a game at a high level, a small detail can make a big difference to its outcome. Applying pressure on a referee during a game may eventually give you one favourable decision, and that single decision could be the difference between winning, drawing or losing the game. Although the Japan national team is known as the 'Samurai Blue' by our native supporters, there may come a time when we need to forget part of *Bushido*, the code of the samurai, if we want to really compete on the world stage.

Of course, we should never cross a line that shouldn't be crossed. We must never try to win dirty. The same applies for supporters. Seeing an opponent as a rival and discriminating against the opposition are two totally different things and there must be no place for the latter on or off the pitch. In Japan, a country that can still be viewed as almost an ethnically homogeneous nation, people may not always be aware of racial discrimination, but once outside the country your eyes are soon opened to its existence as a very sensitive and sad reality.

It wasn't long ago that a South Korean player felt he was racially abused during an international friendly against Colombia, and a Brazilian player playing for J.League side Urawa Red Diamonds in an AFC (Asian Football Confederation) Champions League game held in Saudi Arabia received what appeared to be racially abusive language on social media. I, for one, have received similar messages after playing for Japan in the Middle East. How people who seem to be just local football fans can subject a fellow human being to such abusive language is completely beyond my comprehension.

Thankfully, in English football society, including the Premier League, there seems to be a firm attitude towards racial discrimination. There is also an anti-racist structure in place, with organisations such as Kick It Out working for the eradication of discrimination. Fans know that if someone in the crowd does or says something racially abusive, he or she will be ejected from the stadium and never allowed back.

I also believe that English people in general understand innately where the line that shouldn't be crossed lies, thanks to the dry sense of humour that is so common among them. For example, when we play 'secret Santa' every Christmas at Southampton, the gifts we give each other are rich in humour. Virgil van Dijk once received a Manchester City shirt when he was rumoured to be joining them, although he would eventually leave for Liverpool later. I often receive something stereotypically Japanese or oriental. One year, it was 'Pokémon' (characters from a Japanese video game) goods, and another, it was a kung-fu costume. I remember giving Jay Rodriguez, who went on to join West Bromwich Albion in 2017, a Teenage Mutant Ninja Turtles onesie, as I used to tell him, 'You drive a Ninja Turtle,' whenever I saw him driving his dark green hot hatchback to our training ground. He knew exactly who his secret Santa was as soon as he opened his present!

We all laugh about these jokes as part of our banter among team-mates, but they could be interpreted differently if such gifts were given outside our circle, when they could be seen as discrimination or prejudice. In England, however, most people, including my team-mates, understand where the borderline between black humour and racial abuse lies.

Monsters and aliens

Another aspect of Premier League life is the opportunity you have of meeting 'monsters' and 'aliens'. That was obvious to me from my first year at Southampton. I'm not talking about visiting Loch Ness in Scotland, which is famous for alleged sightings of 'Nessie', or Stonehenge, a massive mysterious prehistoric monument that is only about a one-hour drive away from Southampton. I'm talking about encounters on the pitch.

I have always categorised top-class foreign players in my own way: a player recognised as being integral for a Premier League side is a 'monster', while a world-class player – perhaps a key man at one of the European giants such as Barcelona or Real Madrid, clubs regularly regarded as UEFA Champions League title contenders – is an 'alien'. I used to think such players belonged to another world or planet from mine but, as a Premier League player, I now have a chance to play against them week in, week out.

My first encounter with a 'monster striker' on a Premier League pitch came only a week after I made my début. It was a game at Villa Park where I faced Christian Benteke, who was Aston Villa's centre-forward at the time. He was unbelievably strong in the air. I had played against players who were physically large in the

Netherlands, but marking Benteke made me realise that the Premier League really was in a league of its own, as I had never dealt with anyone as dominant in the air as he was.

Then, the following week, I played against someone with even more physical presence, a 6' 4" and 187 lb midfielder named Marouane Fellaini, then at Everton. He could jump higher in the air than I thought possible, and on the floor his legs could reach where I didn't think they could do, to nick the ball off me.

In those two consecutive physical battles I was elbowed four times in total – three times by Benteke and once, but in the face, by Fellaini – and none of the incidents were ruled a foul by the referee! If my début game for Southampton gave me a 'Welcome to the Premier League' message, teaching me that I'd be punished the moment I switched off, then I received a 'Welcome to the Monsters' Land' message from the tough physical battles of those following two league games.

At the same time, I also started to become aware of a difference between what I thought was a good centre-back and the type of centre-back actually rated in the Premier League.

At that time in Japan, a centre-back who was technically sound or a good reader of the game tended to be more appreciated. In the national team, the first-choice centre-back pairing was Marcus Tulio Tanaka and Yuji Nakazawa, both physically able defenders, but one of their immediate predecessors, who had been seen as the core of Japan's defence line, was Tsuneyasu Miyamoto, who was rated for his football intelligence which compensated for his lack of physical presence.

However, once in the Premier League I quickly realised that physicality was a must for a centre-back. Everyone who was recognised as a good centre-back here seemed stronger than average both physically and mentally. I even felt that you wouldn't be seen as a specialist centre-back, let alone rated as one, if you didn't seem physically strong enough. People think it's a given that a centre-back wins a fifty-fifty ball. The mark of a very strong defender, meanwhile, is that he will win the ball in a challenge in which his chances of doing so are less than 50 per cent. In Japan my physical strength was never questioned, but in England some seemed to see me from the start as slightly built for a centre-back.

I must admit that in England I felt, 'F***, it really hurts,' when I blocked a shot at close range. I'm not saying I didn't feel any pain when I blocked a shot by a Japanese player, but it would usually be just like, 'Ouch'. However, when a shot from a Premier League striker hits you it feels like a heavy body blow. In one of my early training sessions as a Southampton player I nearly doubled up in agony when I caught a powerful shot by Ricky Lambert, who was our main striker at that time. I literally felt the 'power' of the Premier League, and it wasn't even at a game but at our training ground.

People over here may have a fixed image of the Japanese being small, but it is also true that the way defenders in the Premier League defend is actually more forceful than defenders in Japan do, regardless of their physical size. For example, when facing a player on the ball, I believe the majority of defenders in Japan would simply try to delay the opposition's attack by getting tight on the player without actually tackling him. But here in England, after getting tight on the ball player, a defender is more likely to try to win the ball back from him rather than just keep backing off. When contact is made, the tackle itself will also be stronger than the average one in Japan. A Premier League defender puts a player under pressure, as if he is diving right into the opponent's chest. It's just a much more aggressive approach than a J.League defender's. Perhaps the best way to summarise the difference is to say that the way players defend here isn't merely passive but is more proactive.

And that makes the penalty area, usually referred to as the 'box', more like a rectangle-shaped 'ring' for phys-ical combat in a Premier League game. If an averagely built player from an Asian country – let's say less than 5' 9" in height and less than 160 lbs in weight – is in the box trying to compete, it's not a surprise to see him struggle.

You'd think he has virtually no chance to win an aerial battle in the box. There is no time, nor space to run up. He has to try to head the ball from a standing jump, and even that jump needs to be done while pushing and shoving with an opponent who is bigger than him. I'm 6' 2" tall, but in my first season at Southampton it was only natural for me to focus more on covering the space around me while my taller partner Jos, or the sturdier-built José, would attack the ball in the air in a set-play situation in our own box.

At the same time, I also tried to be braver on the pitch. It's not because I was conscious that people here like a brave warrior kind of image, but I felt I should try to avoid showing any pain after a tackle, if it wasn't unbearable, even if the other player looked in pain. I tried to carry on as if it were nothing, putting on a poker face even though inside me I was grimacing with pain. As a real samurai would say, 'Endure with dignity,' though this footballing samurai might sometimes want to say, 'Pain is pain.'

Once you get used to it, you can pretend more naturally. Then your opponents start thinking, 'He's strong.

We won't be beating him with power,' or, 'We should forget about trying to make inroads there.' Your manager would also see that you are strong enough. In England, being strong physically and mentally is a minimum requirement for a centre-back.

On 1 January 2013 I had the chance to face Arsenal for the first time after they had inflicted a heavy defeat on us in my début game for Southampton. For me, this game was like an adaptability test in the Premier League.

Theo Walcott, who scored Arsenal's sixth goal in that first meeting with them, is a forward with threatening pace, and is sometimes dubbed a 'speedster' by the English media. If I call the likes of Benteke or Fellaini a 'power monster', he falls in a 'speed monster' category.

I knew some of the media were using the word 'revenge' for our second encounter with Arsenal that season. But my personal keyword for this game was 'adjust' and, actually, although the game finished 1–1, José and I as a centre-back pair managed to nullify the threat of Walcott by cutting out the supply to him. By adjusting well to Arsenal's pacy attack as a unit, it made me feel confident, too, as I could see I was adapting successfully to the Premier League.

Among those 'monsters' I encountered in my début season in the Premier League, by far the most 'monstrous' was Luis Suárez, the Liverpool striker. The Uruguay international is only a year older than me but he is definitely a player whom I would put in my 'alien' category. I couldn't really read what he was going to do to get past me. He seemed to be equipped with so many options as a striker but, at the same time, he was very single-minded about going towards the goal. He was always ready to attack and constantly thinking what the best way would be to get a goal next time, while I, as a defender facing him, was having a tough time trying to read what he was going to do. In fact, he was scoring at that time no matter whom he was playing against, and that's why he left for Barcelona at the end of the following season as the Premier League top scorer.

British English as my second English language

At my official unveiling as a Southampton player, though it was held five days after my début game, I managed to draw a laugh from local journalists with a joke about British food. But in reality my confidence in my English was at its all-time low after moving from the Netherlands to England: the home of the English language.

Come to think of it, I had hardly ever spoken to native English speakers before I joined Southampton. There were Europeans around me even in the Grampus first team, but Frode Johnsen was a Norwegian striker and

Sef Vergoossen, my first manager there, was a Dutchman, while his successor, Piksi (Dragan Stojković), was a Serbian. They did speak English, but it was a foreign language to them as well.

In addition, the English learned at a Japanese school is American English, and it was only after I came to England that I realised its difference from British English. It almost sounded like a different language to me. The sound of 'r' is not as strong as in American English, while 'h' seems pronounced as 'haich' instead of 'aich' and 'z' is pronounced as 'zed', not 'zee' as we learn in our English class at school in Japan. What was all my hard work in my school days for?

People use different words here, too. A 'flat' is what we know as an 'apartment', and an 'elevator' is called a 'lift'. A pair of 'sneakers' becomes a pair of 'trainers' and a 'sweater' a 'jumper', while what we call a 'trainer' in Japanese-English is a 'sweatshirt' in England. Before I came here, I didn't pay any attention to the note – '(UK)' or '(US)' – that I sometimes saw in my dictionary when I looked up a word, because I didn't understand what exactly the note was there for. But now I do.

One of the mishaps that taught me the difference between '(UK)' and '(US)' was an incident which I recall as the 'omelette with invisible paprika'. One day at the club's canteen I ordered a plate of omelette with ham, cheese and paprika inside, but I couldn't find any paprika when I ate it. It was the same the second and third time I ordered the dish. It had ham and cheese inside but not paprika, or at least not as I recognised it. So I went to ask if my order had been understood properly. To my surprise, the answer was, 'It's there inside.' I double-checked, looking for a piece of paprika inside my omelette using a fork, but without success. Then I went up again to the serving area, this time with a photo I had found on the internet of what I call a paprika, and received another surprising reaction. 'Ah, you mean "peppers",' I was told. I learned that day that what people here call paprika is a reddish powdered spice.

In British English, there are also some words that I personally think should have a '(UK Football)' note attached to them in a dictionary. For instance, when I arrived at Southampton I found what I knew as the 'team bus' referred to as the 'team coach', while the other players were not calling our boss 'the manager' but 'the gaffer'. I really felt I had to start learning another foreign language.

My first 'gaffer', Nigel Adkins, was from Merseyside. Although I didn't find his English so heavily accented, it was still extra hard for me to understand because it was so fast. I now confess that in my early team meetings my head was filled with question marks. If I had to answer something, I said 'Yes' to almost anything on the spot, but then I had to ask a team-mate to explain to me what had been said to me, this time in slower and easier-to-understand English.

On the other hand, my English may also have sounded quite difficult to comprehend to my team-mates and the team staff. It still does sometimes. One embarrassing example is my 'singing début' at Southampton.

In England, many clubs have a custom in which a new player is asked to sing a song in front of the team. It was the same at Southampton, and I had to go through this ritual as well when I joined. It went terribly. It was a day before an away game, and we were having a meal together at the team hotel. I stood up as my team-mate, Kelvin Davis, who was in charge of proceedings, tapped his glass with a fork as a cue for my performance. I was going to sing a Japanese children's song called 'Kaeru no uta' (The Froggy Song). This song is usually sung in a round, meaning everyone sings the same lyrics to the same melody but starts at different times. I wanted to do it the same way, so I explained it to my team-mates, or I thought I did.

But the resulting performance had nothing 'in a round'. Everyone was singing their own made-up lyrics in different melodies at whatever timings they wanted to start singing. Sweating nervously, all I could do was get to the end of the song, ignoring what was going on around me just to finish the ritual.

These days, now I have become one of the old faces in the team, I'm the one to give a cue to new faces performing our ritual. I took the role after Kelvin, our long-serving goalkeeper and club captain, retired in 2016. (He returned to the club as a first team assistant coach in December 2017.) I totally shut my eyes to my disastrous performance back in 2012, and ask a newcomer questions like, 'Do you have a partner?', 'When was the last time you had a date?' before telling my entire audience, 'Now he's going to sing a song for us. Please welcome the one and only Mr John Smith!'

Anyway, I really wonder how I got through my first year without any major incidents in the world of British English.

Looking back now, my English during the press conference for my unveiling or in my early interviews as a Southampton player must have been full of mistakes. But even so, people at the club or in the media didn't see it as a problem. They didn't seem to mind my English. The fact that nobody mentioned how bad it was has made me feel, little by little, more confident to speak the language, rather than worrying unduly about how imperfect it is.

As time went by, I started to think that my English wouldn't have to be perfect in order to carry on my life here. Even if nearly half of what I said was grammatically incorrect, the important thing was getting the basic meaning across. If I want to be more fluent, which I do, I can keep learning and trying to improve my English, again little by little. By improving, one also realises that what we studied at school, basic grammar, wasn't actually pointless.

The fact that I am not a reserved type may also have helped me improve my English. Among my non-English team-mates, it always seems to be someone who is talkative in his native tongue who learns English quickly. As they like talking in general, when they feel frustrated at not being able to say what they want to say, they won't hesitate to ask someone else or check by themselves, and a word or expression you come to learn and use that way straight away sticks much better in your memory.

On the other hand, if you are quite introverted, someone who likes to spend more time looking at your mobile phone in the dressing room, it will be harder to improve your English conversational skills. You just need to make a first step to get into the conversation, even if you know you won't understand much. It can be very heavy going at first, but the more you try, the easier it gets. That much I know from my own experience.

Even with my not-so-shy character, I found getting into a conversation that my team-mates were having quite tough. For a while, I felt I had hit a British English wall shortly after my move to Southampton. I was pleased when they asked me to join them for a meal or event out together, but at the same time I felt it was bit of a hassle because I feared I'd get bored listening to conversations I could not follow.

However, every time I joined in I found myself catching more words and increasingly being able to understand what my team-mates were saying, as my ears were getting used to their voices and the way they spoke English as well. I obviously got closer to them, too, and that meant we had more interesting subjects in common to talk about. Once I started to enjoy simply being with them and having a chat, despite not being able to understand everything, I knew I was getting closer to breaking the wall.

As a centre-back, I needed to be able to communicate in English with my team-mates on the pitch as well. It is often said that football itself is a universal language, but a real language is also necessary in order for a defender to talk football on the pitch. For a player in an attacking position, such as a striker, where your 'sense' can speak volumes, you might get away with only a shout of 'Hey!' or 'Here!' to ask for a pass to do your job.

But the job description of a centre-back involves giving directions to your defensive colleagues, such as, 'Come closer to cover the space here,', 'I go, you cover,', 'Squeeze!' or 'Push up!' You must be able to communicate verbally with the team-mates around you during the game to let them know what you want them to do.

Not only that, you are supposed to do so while your emotions are running high on the pitch. It means, in my case, that I don't really have time mentally to translate from Japanese into English what I want to tell my team-mates. As a result, I found it quite difficult in my first year in England. I was giving instructions to players around me in a foreign language at VVV too, but these were limited to shouting out some simple words, such as 'right', 'left' or 'stop', either in Dutch or English depending on whom I was partnered with in the middle of the back line. But over here, the instructions need to be more precise. In a situation where I just needed to shout 'Behind!' to my team-mate at VVV, I would be shouting, 'Left shoulder!' or 'Right shoulder!' to let my Southampton team-mate know which side he needed to pay attention to. It took me a good year to feel comfortable enough to shout instructions to team-mates around me in English during the game.

Once speaking English became second nature on the pitch, it gave me a few problems. One of them was reacting to something with a swearword without intending to. If you ask me what I most frequently say in English on the pitch, my answer would be 'for f***'s sake'. My team-mates often say that phrase, too. For instance, if one of them leaves his position despite me telling him, 'Stay there!' and our opponent exploits that space to put a pass through, I'll quickly dash to deal with the danger, while shouting, 'For f***'s sake!'

Another situation is when I'm with our national team. I could sometimes be heard shouting something in English to my Japanese team-mates, such as 'Push up!' whereas I could simply say 'Agero!' in Japanese. I always feel a little embarrassed when I realise I've just done that.

Frankly speaking, it's not that easy to switch my brain from 'Premier League mode' to 'Japan national mode' every time I join the national team, as it's usually only for a short period, 10 days or so at the most. I believe my team-mates in the national team who are at overseas clubs will understand. So if there are occasions when you wonder, 'Why the hell is Maya barking at his Japanese team-mates in English?' please just be so kind as to ignore me.

On the other hand, if that makes some of the Japanese supporters think, 'I want to be an English-speaking world citizen some day, just like Maya is trying to be,' I would advise them not to worry about making grammatical mistakes at first. As I've said, I was initially conscious about making mistakes in English, especially as I came to a country where English is the first language. I thought I had to speak in proper English. But at some point I came to realise, as if I had reached enlightenment, that there was no way I would ever speak perfect English and I wouldn't have to. Just reasonable conversational English would do, mistakes and all.

Around me, there were non-English team-mates of mine who also made me feel that way. My French or Italian team-mates speak English with a very strong accent from their mother tongue. Sometimes, what they say includes a word or two from their own language, and it sounds just like they are speaking French or Italian to my ear. But that doesn't make them reluctant to speak English. And that encouraged me to do the same. I tried to communicate in English without worrying too much about making mistakes, but focusing on getting my point across. I still can't say I have completely smashed down the British English wall, but I don't feel nervous or hesitant to have a conversation in English any more.

Even having a dream in English is not unusual for me these days. Once, I was playing a futsal (a version of five-a-side) against Arsenal players inside my elementary-school gymnasium in my dream. I wondered for a moment, 'Am I going to move to Arsenal?', though, of course, there was no way it could be a precognitive dream. I've heard that it's a sign that you've overcome the language barrier when you start having a dream in English. I don't remember at all when I had such a dream for the first time or what it was about. Whatever it was, it was nothing compared to fulfilling my dream of playing in the Premier League when I moved to England.

Christmas 'working' holidays

On 18 January 2013 in a snow-covered London, my mobile phone rang in the morning. It was a text message from the club at an unexpected time, as I was enjoying a rare two days off with my wife and my team-mate, Chung-kun (Tadanari Lee), in London. But the content of the message was even more unexpected. As I opened it, I learned that Nigel Adkins had been sacked by Southampton.

I could say nothing but 'What?' Looking at the view of London all in white, my mind went blank.

There had been rumours about his impending dismissal during the first half of the season. Southampton made a poor start in their first campaign back in the Premier League. The Arsenal game, my first as a Saints player, was a fourth defeat in the opening four league fixtures. We spent most of the first half of the season in the bottom three.

However, when the sacking of the manager became a reality, the team was showing signs of recovery. We were unbeaten in the league for five consecutive games. Only two days before his departure we took a point from Champions League holders Chelsea at their home in a 2–2 draw. We had come out of the relegation zone and were a respectable 15th in the league table by the time the club made the decision.

The fact that Adkins had overseen consecutive promotions, from League One to the Premier League, made the news even more shocking for me. But I had also heard that Mr Nicola Cortese, then the chairman of the club, was a very ambitious man, and maybe he thought he should start preparing for the following season rather than merely avoiding relegation. Digesting the news, I couldn't help but feel how tough it is to survive at the top level, not only for a player but also for a manager.

I then replied to the message, asking who the successor was to be. The answer was, 'Mauricio Pochettino.' Again, I could only react with, 'What?' Nowadays everyone knows him as the manager who turned Tottenham into contenders for the Premier League title, but at that time not many in England had heard about this Argentine manager, who had been with Espanyol in the Spanish La Liga.

For a player, a change of manager means starting all over again to win his trust. Adkins's sacking came only four months after my début at Southampton. There was nothing the players could do once the board had made the decision, but we felt a little uneasy on our return car journey from London, with Chung-kun at the steering wheel, as a potentially slippery road appeared to be ahead of us in more ways than one.

There was also the fact that Adkins, who had brought me to Southampton, was a very positive manager. He projected the air of an educator, reminding me to a certain extent of the first ever manager in my professional career, Sef at Grampus. More than anything, he was the manager who trusted me and played me. It was my very first season in the Premier League and the team had lost by a big margin in the first game I played under him, but he had still said to me, 'Don't worry, son. You go on from here. Next up is the Villa game,' and indeed he kept playing me in the starting 11 from the following week.

I was desperate to repay his trust, and prove myself in the Premier League. I was hell-bent on playing game after game. Looking back now, perhaps I needed to calm down a little. There are many things that I don't remember that well from my first season at Southampton. The year 2012 went like crazy for me, though I didn't feel that way back then.

At the end of the 2011/12 season in the Dutch Eredivisie, I was involved in a relegation play-off against a second division club; then, the following month, I was with the Japan national team to play two 2014 World Cup qualifiers – although it turned out to be just one and a half games to be precise, as I came off in the second game with a knee injury. Once back to a fit enough condition, I was playing in the 2012 London Olympics until the third-/fourth-place decider before going back to the Netherlands to play a league game and then moving to England. Shortly after joining Southampton, I made my début in the first game I was named in a match-day squad and from the next week onwards I was in the starting 11. It was really non-stop for me.

Moreover, there is no winter break in the Premier League, unlike domestic leagues in other European countries such as Spain, Italy, Germany, France and the Netherlands. Christmas holidays in Europe are like the New Year holidays in Japan. It's a holiday period to spend time with your family. For a player, it is also a time to recharge your batteries both mentally and physically after the first half of the season.

However, in England, where I understand that football is part of people's everyday life and has always been the biggest source of entertainment, the league schedule gets busier instead of coming to a break during the festive period! Playing in the Premier League was my dream, but fulfilling that dream involved the reality of working all the way through to the New Year.

However, clubs do still organise Christmas parties in December. At Southampton they decide on a different theme every year and, to me, it's always extra fun to be at a party which seems and feels very European, such as one billed as a James Bond evening and attending the '007 night' in a tuxedo, or going to a masquerade with a mask in hand.

But we don't have actual Christmas holidays. Instead, we have 'working holidays'. With the packed fixture list, I would even call Christmas and New Year 'workaholic holidays'. During my first such holiday period in England, I played full time in four league games and one FA Cup game in the two-week period starting just before Christmas.

And the general 'working conditions' in the English winter alone are quite tough for a footballer. For a country whose latitude is not so different from that of Hokkaido, the northernmost prefecture in Japan which is known for its heavy snowfall, it doesn't snow much here, but it sure can be cold. Sub-zero mornings are the norm. In lower divisions, games can be called off due to a frozen pitch, as some of the stadiums are not as well equipped as those in the Premier League. I later found out that my first winter here was colder than usual, with an average temperature of around just 3° centigrade, and it was the wettest December in more than a decade. In that winter I found it seriously tough to play on New Year's Day with only a two-day interval from the Stoke away match, which was our third game in a week.

Of course I was happy to play game after game, and it's not that I was feeling I had to put a brake on to slow myself down during that period, but, as the second half of the season went on, my body started to creak under the ever-increasing fatigue until, around February, the pain I was experiencing around my groin was becoming too much to ignore.

I have come to realise that some experienced teams or players in the Premier League intentionally slow down the pace of the game during the busy Christmas period, by taking much longer than usual before taking a throw-in or a goal kick to advance the clock, for instance, regardless of the situation in the match or the time left in a game. It's like they are playing in an 'eco-drive' mode, playing for an acceptable result while trying to conserve their energy.

And it makes sense in a way. If you take the busy Christmas period as a small section of a long season, it's not too bad if you take six or seven points in total without putting in too much effort from three league games in a space of seven days. Such an approach could be part of an effective strategy to go through the tough Premier League season and get the result you want at the end.

But for me, in my first season here, I kept driving myself at full throttle, including during the congested period. I kept going even with a hairline fracture of my little toe after the turn of the year. That was an injury I sustained near the end of January during an away game against Manchester United, for whom Shinji (Kawagawa) was playing, when their striker, Robin van Persie, stepped on my foot by accident.

For such an injury on a little toe, it is common practice to wait for it to heal naturally while carrying on playing. I, too, kept playing for a while with a little help from painkillers. I didn't want to put a halt to my playing streak, which had continued even under the new manager. But the pain was there when the effect of the painkillers wore off, and soon I started to feel the pain in my groin, too. It was a physically tough lesson to take in during my first year in the Premier League.

End of my first Premier League season

My personal 2012/13 season in the Premier League opened with the game against Arsenal in mid-September 2012 and ended with the game against West Bromwich in late April 2013, which was league fixture number 35 for Southampton in the season. I sat on the bench for the remaining three league games but I was in no condition to actually come off the bench.

All the same, I could still give my first season at Southampton a pass grade. That's how I felt at the time. I played as the first-choice centre-back and made some contribution to the team, which finished 14th in the league table.

People in the media might have given me a lower grade. But I'm one of those players who hardly takes any notice of what is being said about me by the press and such like, including match reports or player ratings in national newspapers. If a newspaper happens to be there right in front of me, I would understand what is written because it's in English. I sometimes go online to have a casual look at some of the football-related websites such as the Sky Sports home page, where, again, I may see something about us or myself. But even then, I don't really worry about what's being said there. The media's reaction, including that in Japan towards its national team, can go from extreme to extreme. They can be heaping praise on you one moment, and bringing you down the next. There seems no point worrying about it. I know some players and managers do care, but I personally have never seen that sort of attitude guiding them somewhere positive or good. At the end of the day it's all down to individual perspective but, to me, worrying about what others are saying about you or your team seems a waste of energy.

I know what I need to work on to become a better player. I don't need someone else to tell me what I'm lacking or not very good at. As a professional, you should think that way. I was aware, in my first season in the Premier League, of those areas in my game where I needed to improve in order to excel as a defender.

Everyone has his strengths and weaknesses, pluses and minuses as a player. A defender with good technical ability and awareness of the space in and around his own penalty area could be short of physical presence or heading ability, for instance. But if you improve on your weakness up to the level where it is no longer seen as your minus point, then what you already have as your plus point can make you a better-than-average defender, a player with something extra. That thought came to my mind.

In my case, I identified my physical strength as something I definitely needed to improve as a centre-back in the Premier League. I was made fully aware of that fact through my encounters with the 'monsters' on the pitch who were in a different league from the players I'd faced in the Netherlands. I needed and wanted to bring my physical strength up, at least to the average among Premier League centre-backs, and to make myself better than average overall. I kept on playing through my first season here with that thought in my mind.

The biggest lesson I learned the hard way – in my unexpected début game against Arsenal – was how costly one small mistake can be. I made far more mistakes when I was playing first in the J.League, and then in the Eredivisie, without being punished too often.

But it's different in the Premier League. One chance is enough for more capable and ruthless opponents. I knew I had to keep working to improve myself in order to survive in what is generally regarded as the hardest league in the world, and as I finished my first season as a Southampton player I was resolved to do just that in the season ahead.

CHAPTER 4

BATTLE AGAINST ADVERSITY

Grim dawn

At Carrow Road, on 31 August 2013, I marked my one-year anniversary as a Southampton player with a 90-minute stint on the bench at the home of Norwich City. I wasn't even on the bench for the first two league games of the 2013/14 season. I hadn't seen that coming, to be honest, and being left out of the team put me in a sulky mood. In the previous season I'd played 32 league games, the most among our centre-backs, and that fact made it extra hard for me to find myself not even in the match-day squad when the new season started.

Looking back at the situation calmly, I should have tried my utmost to be back in a fully fit condition for my second season here at Southampton. That must also have been the least expected of me by Mauricio Pochettino, the manager who took over the team in the second half of the previous season. But in reality I simply couldn't concentrate on recovering from the groin injury I had been suffering from during the closing stages of the previous season. Once my first Premier League season was finished, I had to play for Japan in a 2014 World Cup qualifier against Australia. There was no way for me to pass up an opportunity to play for my country, even though I was still struggling with the injury. I also didn't want to whine about it as a professional. I don't think there is a single professional footballer in Europe who is completely free from injuries or pain. Besides, I'd had treatment for my groin in England before I flew back to Japan to join my team-mates in the national team.

After our qualification for the World Cup in Brazil was confirmed with a point, which was the minimum requirement from the Australia game, the 2013 Confederations Cup in Brazil was waiting for us. Although we didn't win any games there, playing against some of the world's top teams, such as Brazil in our first game, and then Italy, carried significant meaning for both Japan and myself.

Unfortunately, the pain in my groin was getting more intense. When I joined Southampton's pre-season training after my late off-season holidays I was a player who, from the manager's point of view, was not only starting the pre-season late but also still carrying an injury. I wanted to impress my boss as soon as I joined my Southampton team-mates, but the more I tried, the more pain I felt. As my range of movement decreased, so did my performance level. While Pochettino began work on building his own team for his first full season as the Southampton manager, I was in a situation where I couldn't really complain if he didn't see me as regular starter material during the pre-season.

All the same, I couldn't just accept his judgement quietly. I've always been one to speak out if there is something I need to get off my chest rather than dwelling on it, because I think that's the best way to clear the air. Anyway, Pochettino had already said, 'My door is always open,' in front of the team.

'I shall go and talk to him as he's said he'd welcome that,' I thought. However, the actual conversation didn't turn out the way I hoped.

'If I was to pick you, who do you suggest I omit from the match-day squad instead?' the manager said to me when I asked him why I wasn't picked. He parried my question with one of his own, and my answer was, 'That's not for me to decide. It's your decision, boss.' Then he answered straight back this time, 'That's right. It's my call. And you're not in.'

I just didn't know what to say any more. It was quick and brutal. Leaving the manager's room felt like tasting an instant defeat in a battle of wills. I joked, somewhat piqued, 'Lads, his door's open but it looks like his ears aren't,' to some of my team-mates who were still hanging around at our training centre.

In my mind at that time, I'd been a regular starter until only a few months previously. I was confident that I could keep on doing my job for the team on the pitch. Pochettino himself had continued to play me after he took over the team during the second half of the previous season. So why not this season? 'Why?' I kept telling myself. 'I can prove that I'm good enough if only he gives me a chance,' but it just made my frustration bigger as the weeks went by in the new season without me playing a Premier League match.

Darkness setting in

It felt like an eternity. One month, two months, three months went by without me starting in a league game. I had to wait until the match against Aston Villa on 4 December 2013 until I finally made the starting 11 in a league game in my second year at Southampton.

And it didn't go well. In just the 15th minute after kick-off I let Gabriel Agbonlahor, whom I thought I had under my watch, run into the space behind me too easily, and the Aston Villa striker opened the scoring. I wanted to show the manager that I could compete to win my place back, but instead it was as though my display on the pitch was signalling to him that I wasn't even ready to fight for a starting role. Being rusty due to a lack of playing time could never be an excuse for a player in the situation I was in. I had just allowed our opponents to score from a counter-attack that hadn't at first seemed especially dangerous, and it was more down to my lack of concentration than to there being a big space behind our defensive line.

Nonetheless, early in the second half of the season I was given a run of games. It was due to the absence of Dejan Lovren, who had become our first-choice centre-back since his move from Lyon in the summer but had then damaged an ankle ligament towards the end of the Sunderland game on 18 January 2014. I felt for Dejan but was determined to make the most of this unexpected opportunity, thinking, 'I've been doing what I'm supposed to do to be ready. Now is my chance to turn the situation around.'

After spending a few minutes on the pitch as a replacement for the injured Dejan in the Sunderland game, I was in the starting line-up against Arsenal in the following league fixture. Throughout the 90 minutes, from which we took a point off a superior side, I felt, 'At last I'm getting the joy of playing back.' We followed a 2–2 draw against Arsenal with two wins and two draws, and I thought I had put in a decent shift in those five games I started.

But a string of decent performances wasn't enough to win my place back properly. That was the harsh reality, and it was the West Ham away game on 22 February 2014 that turned out to be the key match in my second year at Southampton.

We lost 3–1, but the actual game wasn't as one-sided as the scoreline suggests. We even took the lead early in the first half. And it was my goal – my first Premier League goal! I'd finished the previous season without a single goal to show in the league despite playing regularly. I know I'm a defender but going through more than a season without a league goal was a new – and not especially enjoyable – experience for me.

I found it difficult to break my duck in the Premier League. In a set-piece situation the physical battle inside the box is much harder than anywhere else I have experienced. Sometimes it is like being in a grappling fight. Also, in my first season at Southampton I wasn't yet recognised as one of the key target men by my teammates, so corner kicks and free kicks were rarely aimed at me. I felt, therefore, that the best I could contribute to my team's chances of scoring was by taking a supporting role, blocking an opponent's path, for instance, so that our target man could meet the cross. The most realistic way for me to get my name on the scoresheet, I decided, was to hide behind someone taller than me as the ball was crossed and then sneakily get to the loose ball in the crowded box.

When I actually scored my first Premier League goal I just thought, 'Phew, finally!' It was a feeling more of relief than excitement. The lads came dashing towards me to congratulate me but I didn't do a special goal celebration myself. I usually do, though. On English soil, I had delighted the people watching back in Japan by performing the 'Me! Me! Me!' routine (pointing at my face with my thumbs up, one after the other), which I borrowed from a Japanese comedian's signature move to celebrate my goal in the 2012 London Olympic quarter-finals against Egypt at Old Trafford (although, bizarrely, a foreign journalist asked me, 'Were you mimicking King Kong pounding his chest?' after the game).

When a goal is scored it's the most exciting moment in a game of football, and I always want to celebrate the joy it creates among the fans with a memorable action if I'm the scorer. Oka-chan (Shinji Okazaki) often says to me in a joking way, 'No other defenders can come up with such goal celebrations on the spot like you,' though as Leicester's Japanese striker knows, when I'm playing regularly I do usually plan the way I'm going to celebrate my next goal.

If I'm playing week in, week out, and in good form both physically and mentally, I think a bit about how I'll celebrate as part of my preparation for the next game. At that time, however, because I had gone so long without scoring, and more to the point, since I was struggling with the fact that I was getting so few minutes on the pitch in my second season, there had been no room in my mind for thinking about my goal celebration before that West Ham game.

The goal itself was almost forgotten in the end, too, as we ended up losing. I was one of our defenders who couldn't protect the lead. I was in a position where I should have cleared the rebound in the box when West Ham scored their second goal that was on the borderline between offside and onside. We conceded the third from a cross, our defence being completely disorganised. And by this game, Dejan – a Pochettino signing – was almost ready and back on the bench after recovering from his ankle injury.

Dejan joined Southampton in June 2013 while I was away with the Japan national team. Although, as I've said, Southampton has traditionally been a selling club, it does also have a reputable scouting structure and almost always brings in sound replacements, not necessarily internationally established names but players with the ability and potential to establish themselves at Premier League level.

Dejan was the first real new competition I faced as a Southampton centre-back. The arrival of the Croatia international defender wasn't such big news in England.

I didn't know how good he was, either. He was a year younger than me and looked to have a similar build to mine. But my perception of him changed drastically once the season began and he started playing. I soon felt he was one of the best centre-backs in the Premier League, let alone in our squad at that time. He was especially strong in one-on-one situations and was equally impressive with the ball, distributing it effectively after stopping the opponent and winning back possession. He produced performances full of confidence in both defending and attacking week in, week out. It was hardly a surprise when Liverpool came for him after just one season with a transfer bid that was more than twice as much as Southampton had originally paid to Lyon.

Dejan's outstanding form meant I had to be realistic and compete for the remaining place in the middle of the back line, but José (Fonte), who started the season as Dejan's centre-back partner, was also in very good form. Watching them performing perfectly in tune with each other from the bench, I sometimes felt that there was no way for me to get back into the starting line-up. I had already been behind them in the manager's pecking order before the season started, and had still been unable to produce convincing performances during the little time that season I was given on the pitch. The manager must have had every reason not to play me and none not to regard Dejan and José as his regular centre-backs.

I was going to finish my second season at Southampton without a single start after the defeat at West Ham. It was the beginning of by far the darkest and longest period of my football life.

Welcome to the dark side

For a footballer, nothing frustrates one more than not being involved in a match. It's beyond one's imagination. I had a quite long period during which I was unable to play in my first year in the Netherlands, but that was down to injury and two subsequent operations, so at least I knew why I wasn't involved. But it was different this time in my second year in England. I still wasn't playing even after the groin pain had gone. I was fit enough to play, yet I wasn't getting anywhere near enough minutes on the pitch. I had never felt so frustrated for so long.

I kept telling myself, 'I must be patient,' but it didn't help at all. I just didn't know what to do to deal with this new situation for me. I really thought I was going to lose my mind. Certainly, I had already lost sight of my resilience at that time, I believe.

There must be many people who find themselves unde-servingly facing adversity in their career; dismissed, perhaps, from his or her position by a superior without warning or reason. Some might fairly have said to me at that point, 'Your situation is nothing because you're still picking up a fat salary by sitting on the bench.'

But for a footballer, playing in a match is everything. You don't get any satisfaction or meaningful experience out of being on the bench. And the longer you're there, the less you may be figuring in your manager's plans. I wasn't even on the bench in 10 out of 19 league games in the first half of that season.

If you fail to make a match-day squad for a home game, you end up watching the game from the stands. When that happened to me, I must say I was struck again by the passionate atmosphere at a Premier League game, thinking, 'This is great. You've got to be impressed.' But I only felt like that the first few times. Occasionally, with a view of the whole pitch in front of me, I tried to simu-late the game in my head while watching from the main stand at St Mary's. But after a while I started feeling frus-trated, as all I could do was simulate, not actually play on the pitch.

In the case of an away game, all you can do is watch the game on television. Your existence becomes more like that of a fan, rather than a player. I'm a footballer. A professional one. I want to do the job I love. That feeling gave me a false sense of hope that I might be in the squad for the next game, and I ended up getting downhearted, finding out 'I'm not in' time and time again.

Now I'm in a position to say that, despite the frustration I endured, that period taught me the importance of patience. But I didn't have enough patience at that time. All I had inside me was an ever-increasing anxiety about how long the situation would continue.

When I was in the Netherlands and sidelined with my metatarsal injury, I tried to take a good hard look at myself by having an internal dialogue in my flat with the light switched off. It was around five months after the operation, and I was starting to feel increasing anxiety on top of my frustration, as the pain in my left foot didn't seem to be going away, even after I'd been through the rehabilitation process.

Then I was dealt another blow when I went back to Japan, initially for treatment for my injury. At a Japanese hospital I was told that another operation would be necessary. That meant I would be out for another five months, and that was too much for me to take at that time. I'm quite a positively minded person, for whom a single good night's sleep is usually enough to forget about some disappointment or sorrow. But the day I heard that diagnosis from a Japanese surgeon I just couldn't sleep at all. The prospect of a second operation and another extended period of rehabilitation seemed a far tougher and longer ordeal – one that I'd surely struggle to get through.

One day while in Japan I visited my wife Miku, then still my girlfriend. I was having another sleepless night, and when I sat up in bed I realised she was also still awake, and weeping silently beside me. Despite my unconvincing efforts to put on a brave face in front of her, she must have understood how devastated I was at being struck down with an injury right after my first move abroad. She was crying as she felt my pain inside her, too.

We didn't say a word to each other in that moment, though we both knew we were still awake. During that silence it felt as if the fog was clearing in my head and I just felt, 'I'm going to spend my life with this person,' deep in my heart. And my feeling was right.

At Southampton, whenever I come home I know Miku will be waiting for me. Since we've been together for more than a decade now, she knows a thing or two about football, but she's always the same when she welcomes me back after a game, regardless of whether or not I was involved in it, and the result.

The sense of security and comfort that her warmth provides has added a new ingredient to my resilience that I didn't have when I was living alone in the Netherlands.

Enjoying her tasty and healthy home-cooked meals has helped give me the strength to carry on, too. I so enjoy her cooking that my answer would have to be 'All of them' if I was asked to pick my favourite from her recipes. She cooks a variety of dishes for our dinner every day and I know that's no easy task. The lower I felt, the deeper my gratitude became for her being with me. In England, even though I was facing the toughest time ever in my football career, I could always come home to warmth and comfort.

However, I felt as though I was surrounded by darkness at Southampton. I lost my compatriot, Chung-kun (Tadanari Lee), as he was on his way out of St Mary's, released by the club after making only two League Cup appearances in the first half of the season. As for my other team-mates, many of the first-team regulars were on a steep upward trajectory, such as Dejan, Ricky Lambert and Adam Lallana, who would all start the following season as Liverpool players, and Luke Shaw, who was going to move to Manchester United at only 18 years of age. Southampton, who would finish the season eighth in the league table, six places higher than the previous season, were also upwardly mobile as a club.

On the other hand, I felt that I'd fallen as low as I'd ever imagined I could. I felt as though I was standing on the outside looking in. During my first year at

Southampton I'd enjoyed joining my team-mates off the pitch, but now I realised that I had even lost my appetite for being one of the lads.

While I wasn't getting many opportunities to express my personality on the pitch, I was also losing my personality off the pitch on my way to the dark side. There was one thing I began to see – the brutal reality of my second year in the Premier League. It made me feel so insignificant.

It made me doubt myself, too. I wasn't a good enough player to make a centre-back's position my own at Southampton. I wasn't sufficiently strong mentally to man up, either. This harsh realisation pushed me even further into the darkness. I thought I had already faced up to some tough aspects of reality, such as the fierce competitiveness of the professional football world or the merciless nature of the Premier League. But now I had to face the stark reality of my own personal crisis. Dealing with that would be the biggest challenge of my career so far.

Pitch-darkness

By the time the 2013/14 season moved into its second half, things went from bad to worse for me. I went from sulking to panicking. During what turned out to be the longest period on the bench in my playing career thus far, I had become so desperate that I no longer understood what I should do to put myself back into the manager's plans and what he would want to see from me when I was given a chance to play.

Moreover, when I was given a rare opportunity I found there was a gap between the picture of things I had in my head and my resulting action. Perhaps partially because of the fact that I went into the pre-season carrying an injury, coupled with the lack of playing time to get match fit, what I could physically do was not up to the standard of what my football brain or senses told me to do. I was sometimes beaten in a situation where I thought I couldn't be beaten. I often failed to make a pass which I thought I could. From outside, I'm sure I looked like someone being beaten too easily or making silly mistakes. The harder I tried, the more individual errors I made. I ended up showing my desperation, not my ability, on the pitch, which I believe just removed me even further away from the manager's thinking.

When a footballer is playing week in, week out and feeling that he is in good form, everything becomes easy. He can control the ball instantly without thinking too much about his touch. When making a pass, his foot always makes a proper connection with the ball. His head remains clear even if his body gets tired towards the end of the game, so he rarely makes a wrong choice throughout the 90 minutes. When a footballer is in good condition, including his match fitness, he can naturally show what he is all about on the pitch.

I was the complete opposite of such a player at that time. The belief that I had to play well led me to make unnecessary mistakes. Then, focusing on not making mistakes led to different errors because I wasn't paying enough attention to the game. I was caught in a vicious circle on the pitch. My head was full of negative thoughts, such as, 'It may be game over for me if I fail to grab this opportunity,' or 'One more mistake, I'll be a goner.' Being in such an unstable state of mind, I kept making foolish mistakes. There was even a time when I felt on the pitch, 'I'm becoming a bad player.'

As I was making more obvious gaffes, the kind of mistakes duly punished by opponents, I understood that I had become an error-prone defender in some people's eyes, including elements of the British media and my own Southampton supporters. Then the frustration and desperation I was feeling started to turn into a sense of urgency, but at the same time I felt it was a little too late to start climbing up the pecking order in the team. The season was already well into its second half.

There was the 2014 World Cup to come after that season. My first ever World Cup. Or rather, it would be if I received a call-up. The reality was, though, that the key members of the Japan national team at that time were mostly players with clubs outside Japan – a group of players referred to as *Kaigai-gumi* (overseas bunch) by the nation.

I am one of those players. Japanese people see me as a 'Japanese Premier Leaguer'. The reality, though, was that I was a Japanese player who wasn't really playing in the Premier League during that season. The huge gap between people's expectations of me in Japan and the reality I was experiencing in England was very hard for me to cope with.

The Japan manager at that time, Alberto Zaccheroni, trusted me and had played me regularly. I wanted to repay his faith through my performances for the team, and I did try. But it wasn't easy, and I knew it. It was unrealistic to expect my performance level to rise dramatically in those few weeks with Japan after a season of non-regular football at the club.

Even in Japan, some started voicing their concerns that one of the *Kaigai-gumi*, who was not actually getting games at his club, might be selected ahead of someone playing regular football, overseas or otherwise. If someone had put a microphone in front of me at that time and asked, 'What do YOU think?', I would have had to say, 'I totally agree.'

Did I not think about moving to another club to get more games in the season leading up to the World Cup? Well, it's not that I never considered it. But I was in only my second year in the Premier League, my ultimate goal as a footballer since my teenage years. I didn't want to give up my dream too easily after just a six-month-or-so period of life on the bench.

Besides, Southampton effectively had only three first-team centre-backs at that time – the regular pair of Dejan and José, with myself as a back-up. After me there was only Jos Hooiveld, at the age of 30, whose appearances were even more limited than mine. I was actually told by the club that they would be reluctant to let me leave during the January transfer window in 2014.

On the other hand, I wasn't allowed to leave the bench that often, either. I really felt there was no way out of the darkness.

Looking back, I can now see that I failed to do anything constructive to get out of the situation I was in back then. I thought I was trying my hardest, but in reality I was just struggling desperately. Consumed by the darkness, I could not see what I should be doing to get out, nor even what I was actually doing.

To add insult to injury, I damaged my left knee at the training ground in the latter half of March. Right there and then, my second season at Southampton finished, a month earlier than my first season, to my huge disappointment.

New boss, new rival

On 16 June 2014 Ronald Koeman became the new manager of Southampton. The appointment was made when I was in Brazil, playing in the World Cup for Japan. His predecessor, Pochettino, had left the club for Tottenham in the previous month, shortly after the 2013/14 season finished. He was headhunted after guiding Southampton to a top-10 finish with his brand of hard-pressing football in his first year in the Premier League.

From my experience, as one of the old faces at Southampton, it's not only players who have been coming and going at St Mary's; a change of manager is also almost like an annual event here. Mark Hughes, who took over the team towards the end of the 2017/18 season in which I renewed my contract for the second time, was my sixth manager in my sixth year at the club.

Southampton are a relatively small club in Premier League terms. It's significant, I think, that I know by name the majority of the people working for it. Small and friendly it may be, but I have still needed to adapt almost every year since my arrival here to life under a new regime.

In a corporation or organisation away from football, there are also changes of personnel at management level but I doubt as frequently as almost every year. The manager of the first team is an extremely important position at a football club, since the team's success on the pitch affects the club's commercial success significantly. For us players, meanwhile, the manager is our immediate superior who has our fate in his hands.

Having said that, for players who have no choice but to accept a managerial change, it may turn out to be a blessing in disguise, as it can give them the sense of a fresh start. Whatever your occupation, if you are in the same environment for a long time, there is always a danger that everything becomes routine and you find it all too predictable. It's the same for a football player playing under the same manager year after year. One day he may lose that sense of excitement, as he knows more or less what to expect from one day to the next.

By contract, a player like myself at Southampton can be kept on their toes nearly every summer, wondering where and how they will spend the pre-season under the new regime or what aspects of team training the new manager puts the most emphasis on. Under Pochettino, on one occasion we all had to walk barefoot over hot stones during the pre-season camp. It was supposed to be a mind–body practice but it felt more like a scene from a kung-fu movie. As if I was a Shaolin monk lacking total self-discipline, I burned my feet a little. With Koeman we had another quite unique session, in which players had to catch a team-mate falling backwards from about two metres high. This exercise was meant to strengthen the trust among us but we seriously feared for our own safety when Fraser Forster, our giant goalkeeper, was falling down from above.

Regular managerial changes also mean you get to experience the various coaching and man-management styles of managers of different nationalities. This can be beneficial for a player not only in terms of developing his career but also in helping him to grow as a person, picking up insights and good habits from others.

From my own perspective, I was in a situation where starting afresh with a clean slate was very much welcome as I went into my third year at Southampton. It gave me new hope and motivation to escape from the darkness I had fallen into the previous season.

The new boss, Koeman, was a former defender who was known for his vision and ability on the ball under Johan Cruyff at Barcelona. I had an optimistic feeling that I might have more of a chance under this new Dutch manager – who'd come to Southampton after finishing his contract at Feyenoord in his native country – than under the previous regime with an Argentine manager who came here via Spain. For that reason, I strongly felt it was all the more important for me not to repeat the same mistake I had made the previous year.

That's right. I couldn't fall behind during the pre-season again. Never.

As a result, my off-season holiday before my third season at Southampton was the shortest ever for me as a professional player. A three-week summer break is common among players over here, but before joining the first pre-season under Koeman I took only two weeks off – and that included travelling back from the World Cup. I felt I had to hit the ground running in front of the new manager from the first day of the pre-season, even if it meant cutting my summer holiday short by a week. It turned out to be a sacrifice worth making, as I was able to start the season in very good physical condition.

Our opening game was away to Liverpool. Dejan, who had been a team-mate only two months ago, was in the middle of our opponents' back line, while I was the Southampton centre-back replacing him in our starting line-up. Sadly we lost 2–1 at Anfield, making a losing start to the new season, but individually I was happy with the way I started my third season – playing every minute in the first four games, including one in the League Cup during the opening month. I thought I glimpsed a tiny light at the end of the long tunnel.

However, I was at Southampton, a club known for being expert at bringing in new recruits and, of course, they soon brought a centre-back to fill the vacancy after Dejan's departure. The latest player to become my competition was Toby Alderweireld, a Belgium international who joined from Atlético Madrid on a season-long loan.

I knew Toby from my days in the Netherlands when he was playing for Ajax while I was at VVV. I believed that we both had our own attributes and could each contribute to the team in our own way. The media saw it differently, assuming I would be back-up for Toby and would soon be back on the bench following his arrival. But in the end there wasn't a big difference in terms of the number of league games we both played. It was 26 for Toby and 22 for me. In my mind we both played regularly, with neither of us being first choice ahead of the other.

Centre-back/full-back

To be more precise, my 22 league appearances included some games where I was deployed as a full-back, either on the right or the left. I was so desperate to leave my miserable life on the bench behind that I was ready to grab any opportunities coming my way with both hands.

Playing as an emergency full-back was rather welcome for me at that time.

Koeman, who would be headhunted by Everton after two seasons at Southampton, was a very proud manager and had his own way of doing his job. When our full-backs were injured, one after the other, forcing the manager to think about alternatives, he came to me and said, 'You must show me you can play full-back as well.' I found it quite a unique way to stimulate a player. And my answer was, 'Of course!' In my head, in that time of desperation, I interpreted his words as, 'I shall give you a chance to start the game.'

I was prepared for the switch to some extent because there didn't seem to be other candidates to fill the full-back's role in the squad, or a youngster to be promoted. Then, in a training session during which we were practising crossing the ball, I surprised myself by putting in crosses with near pinpoint accuracy! 'It could really be me,' I thought, and I was right.

At first, I was prepared to have a real go at being a full-back, thinking that I should try to win the position, rather than filling it temporarily, with the help of my resilience and ability to adjust to a new environment. However, it didn't take long to realise there was no chance of seeing the birth of 'Maya Yoshida, the regular Southampton full-back' ...

Being two-footed, I think I'm quite a flexible player in terms of positions I can play, but I'm certainly not as adaptable as making a full-back's position my own in the Premier League. The distance a player is supposed to cover in 90 minutes is hugely different between a centre-back and a full-back. And if I'd played as a merely defensive full-back, sitting deep most of the time, I wouldn't have been much use in terms of team tactics.

Under Koeman, we mixed up our attacking style, breaking up passing movements with a direct approach and using long balls if a situation called for it. When that happened, the full-backs needed to be one of the main sources of crosses aimed at the head of our centre-forward by making overlapping runs. If the club had put out an ad to recruit a full-back at that time it would have read, 'Wanted! Someone with great stamina for running up and down along the touchline for 90 minutes.'

As for me, a centre-back, I may sprint back to my usual position after a set-play situation around the opponent's penalty area, but I usually don't have to be running up and down the length of the pitch during the course of the game. I might have a decent ability to put crosses in, but I found I definitely didn't have the legs for running up and down to attack and defend, in order to be our long-term full-back.

During the Chelsea game around halfway through my third season at Southampton, I was shown a yellow card for a foul in my role as an emergency full-back. It was on Eden Hazard, whom I faced as a right-back in that game. Chelsea's playmaker, who scored their equaliser with a piece of individual skill, was only 23 years of age at that time but was already a player who fitted into my 'monster' category. I felt I had to stop the brilliant dribbling wizard illegally as a last resort. After kicking his leg, I said, 'Sorry mate, but you're too quick!', and the little speed monster replied with a wry grin.

Some players are too stubborn to say 'sorry' on the pitch, perhaps because they think it would be interpreted as a sign of weakness to apologise to an opponent during the heat of battle. On the other hand, I once heard somewhere that the English word we Japanese use most frequently when abroad is 'sorry'. As far as I'm concerned, I have no problem with saying 'sorry' to my opponent if I've fouled him and know I was at fault.

All in all, accepting the role of auxiliary full-back gave me more than simply time on the pitch. It helped to improve me as a centre-back as well, since it added another facet to my play.

For example, I now know that, as a centre-back, I should avoid making a pass that bounces when I feed the ball to our full-back. Position-wise, a full-back wants to receive the ball while looking ahead to advance in the initial phase of the build-up. But if my pass bounces, he needs to look down at his feet even if just momentarily to control the ball, and that makes it difficult for him to move onto the next passage of play instantly. It may also force him to make a back pass under pressure from an opponent. So it is a centre-back's responsibility to be careful when feeding the ball to a full-back.

The same applies to the spin of the ball when passing. If I am to feed the ball to our right-back, putting a clockwise spin means the ball will be spinning towards the receiver who is waiting for the pass on my right-hand side. But if spinning counter-clockwise, after his first touch the ball might roll in the direction of an opponent closing in on him. If it's hit with a good pace, the ball spinning from right to left may suit a right-back, enabling him to go forward with one touch of the ball to take advantage of the speed of the pass; on the other hand, it may cause them to lose the ball to an opponent right away. My experience as a full-back has inclined me to hit the ball firmly with topspin or use my left foot to give the ball a clockwise spin when I pass the ball to our right-back to start a build-up.

I like to think that my experience as a full-back has enhanced my game as a centre-back, giving me a deeper appreciation of the needs of my team-mates and making me easier to play with.

Most formidable competition

As I had been playing more games than in the previous season, I started to feel, towards the end of my third season at Southampton, that I was finally crawling back up to winning a regular place in the starting 11. It helped that I remained injury-free, unlike the previous two years when my season had ended prematurely due to a groin injury in the first season and one to my knee in the second.

At the same time, a realistic and constructive approach was going to be adopted to my drive to win back a regular place in the centre of defence. I came to realise that the sheer desperation which I had been close to in the previous season would have to go and be replaced by a determination to build up my strength, and I would start hitting the gym around three times a week in the coming 2015/16 season.

I had done some weight training in previous seasons as well. In my second year here under Pochettino, whose regime is known for hard training, we all sometimes spent an hour or so in the gym before doing the team training sessions for another hour. But I had never been a regular visitor to the gym with a step-by-step plan developed under the guidance of the club's sport scientist, setting a target for each three-month period to improve my physical strength.

My new training programme didn't mean I immediately saw steady progress being made towards the end of the tunnel. A person's physical condition is not something that can be changed or improved overnight. In fact, while I continued my endeavour to gradually improve my strength and fitness, my 20 league appearances in my fourth season at Southampton included only 10 starts, which was down by eight games from the previous 2014/15 season. As a team, we came sixth in the table, the highest finish in the club's history in the Premier League era, but individually I couldn't yet climb up the pecking order to be a regular starter again.

Heading into the new season with the same manager as the previous year for the first time since my move here, a new centre-back was joining the club in the summer of 2015. Not only that, it was the strongest competition I had ever had the privilege to face in the team this time.

Toby Alderweireld had chosen to join Pochettino's Tottenham at the end of the season, but Koeman managed to bring in Virgil van Dijk from Celtic on the last day of the summer transfer window in 2015. The

Dutch international was a 'different class', I thought. Although three years younger than me, I felt he had the potential to be playing at clubs like Real Madrid or Barcelona. He would later join Liverpool for £75 million, a world record for a defender, after two and a half seasons at Southampton.

Over 6' 3" and 200 lbs, Virgil undoubtedly has the body of a 'physical monster'. Not only that, he had the pace to be in the top-three fastest among the Southampton players, including the forwards and wingers, and impressive technique with his feet. Definitely an 'alien' in my own player categorisation. Needless to say, he hits accurate long passes with ease.

Whether it's Steven Gerrard in his playing days or Virgil as my Southampton team-mate, every time I see someone hitting a long ball so accurately, I can't help but be genuinely impressed. I think it's mainly down to the fact that they were brought up in a football culture in which that sort of play was always a part of the game, and by testing themselves from a young age they had become confident enough to kick long balls.

In Japan a style of football based on short passes on the floor has always been the norm. The Spanish tiki-taka style of football represented by Barcelona was emphasised, while effective use of long balls has been pushed aside. Therefore, traditionally, the ability and technique to hit accurate long passes has not been regarded as something necessary for players in Japan.

Virgil's quality as a player, though, is about much more than his ability to hit long balls. He is strong but also quick and technically sound, and he can take the leadership as well.

I aimed to secure a regular place in the team as Virgil's centre-back partner, but I couldn't get more games than the previous season. In the last 10 league games in the 2015/16 season I made only three substitute appearances, partially because of my involvement with the national team in the 2018 World Cup qualifiers in Japan.

Nevertheless, in my fourth season at Southampton I at least had a proper thought-out plan to improve my physical strength, so that, after being sat on the bench, I could positively turn my frustrated energy into beads of sweat in the gym, rather than allowing it to become pent up within. My aim had always been to become a better-than-average Premier League centre-back by working on my minuses as a player so that my pluses would stand out as something extra. In my first year at the club I didn't have enough capacity both physically and mentally to execute the plan. In my second year I lost sight of its necessity when I lost my starting place.

In 2016, as I was heading into my fifth year at Southampton, although I still hadn't managed to win back a regular place, the hands that had been gripping the bars of the training machines in the gym were beginning to push open a door to exit from the darkness.

CHAPTER 5

ARMOUR OF FORTITUDE

Tiny light

The English winter feels long and depressing. It's still dark after seven in the morning, and it's already dark before five in the afternoon. Sunny winter days are rare, unlike in Japan. The clouds hiding the sun seem so low that I feel I can almost touch them. Sometimes, the daytime here looks more like a dusk lasting for several hours.

It was 6 February 2016, on the day of a home game against West Ham. The floodlights at St Mary's Stadium were on from more than an hour before kick-off at 5.30 p.m. To me, it seemed a proper night game rather than a late-afternoon kick-off. On top of that, it was raining in Southampton. The wind had picked up a little, too, by the time the game started. It was a game in a very English winter setting.

On the pitch during that West Ham game, in which I started for the first time in nine league games, I finally thought I saw light far ahead at the end of the tunnel that, funnily enough, I had first entered after the game against the same opposition two years before.

The light was tiny, and it certainly wasn't enough for me to feel I was anywhere near the exit yet. However, I felt that I was beginning to finally make progress. At least, that's how I felt right after the game. I played my first 90 minutes in a league game in almost two and a half months and, just as importantly, helped the team to record a win with a clean sheet. That game against West Ham, the game which gave me hope and then despair as it turned out, stands out as the key match in the prelude to my professional career comeback.

I had a hunch that I might have a chance of starting the game before finding it out for sure the day before kick-off. Ronald Koeman, our manager at that time, had started using a system with three at the back as a tactical option in his second season at Southampton. In theory, that system would increase the likelihood of me, the third-choice centre-back in the team, making the starting line-up. Being two-footed, I am comfortable enough on the ball to play anywhere along our back three – another advantage. Thinking in that positive way, I perceived West Ham not as the team that had been instrumental in pushing me into the darkness by beating us previously, but as the one against whom I had scored my first ever Premier League goal.

And my gut feeling turned out to be true. I scored the only goal of the game in the ninth minute of the first half. The ball from Victor Wanyama, who went on to join Tottenham after the end of the season, found its way into my path slightly fortuitously, and I smashed it home from close range. Perhaps it was more difficult not to score from so near the goal, but I nonetheless celebrated the third Premier League goal in my career, nearly 14 months after my second against Everton at home, with a knee slide on the wet pitch towards a corner flag. The stand in front of me was full of cheers and applause from the Saints faithful and, behind me, my centre-back colleague Virgil van Dijk came running over and gave me a celebratory hug with that muscular upper body of his.

For me, what was even more pleasing than the excitement of scoring a winning goal was the feeling I had as a player, 'Maybe I can go on from here.' The 1–0 win, playing with 10 men for nearly 40 minutes of the second half after Victor Wanyama was sent off, was really a victory of resilience for both the team and myself.

West Ham in the 2015/16 season were tough opponents. They finished the league seventh in the table, with only a point less than us in sixth position. Our league positions were the other way around when we went into the game on the day.

Against us, they played the small but pacy Enner Valencia up front, who was in good form with four goals in the previous four games. On the wings, they had Michail Antonio, a powerful dribbler on one side, and the energetic Victor Moses on the other flank. Dimitri Payet, whose individual skills made him one of the stars of the Premier League at the time, was roaming behind their striker. Shortly after we went a man down, they reinforced their front line by bringing on the giant Andy Carroll, who seemed like a throwback to the days when centre-forwards bullied defenders with their aggression and physical power.

But we coped well with all their threats. Even with 10 men, it wasn't like we simply persevered through the remaining period. We never really had our backs against the wall, and our manager praised our 'calm defensive display' after the game.

Surely, I must have been one of those who defended well. Yet mI found myself back on the bench the follow-ing week. In fact, I was going to end up making only 10 starts in the league with as many substitute appearances in the 2015/16 season – my fourth season at Southampton.

It was an utter shock. I couldn't help thinking that the light I thought I saw, though tiny and far away, was once again little more than an illusion caused by my own wishful thinking. I was almost dismayed. But then again, I just couldn't let myself fall back down to the bottom of the darkness again in the way I did in my second season here. I never, ever wanted to go back to that horrible place.

My performance in the West Ham game wasn't an illusion. From the weather to the tightly contested nature of the game, in that typically English 90 minutes against West Ham on that day I was neither overpowered nor outpaced. That was one encouragement which helped me to keep believing that I should be able to more than compete if I could raise the level of some areas in my game up to the standard here and improve what I had always been good at as a defender. I also knew through my experiences that it would be easier said than done, but the more I thought about it the more I became convinced that executing the plan to do just that would be my only way to get back to being a Southampton regular and surviving in the Premier League. During my fourth season, even though I was still quite a way off from the end of the tunnel, it became clearer that I simply had to make the greatest possible effort in doing what I should be doing.

Tailor-made suit of armour

Every time I see a photo of myself taken when I joined Southampton in 2012, I can't help thinking, 'I was thin (and young!).' I have always been considered big among

Asian centre-backs, but over here I was thin, if not small, compared to other Premier League centre-backs. But following the execution of my plan, very slowly but steadily, I began to find myself not getting bumped off as easily or as often as I used to in fifty-fifty situations during training sessions or in actual games.

My plan was to improve my physical strength, which wasn't considered sufficient for a centre-back at Premier League level, so that I could turn my attributes, such as my mobility and agility, into a real advantage. Fortunately, or unfortunately depending on the way I looked at the situation I was in, I had plenty of time to spend in the gym. So I decided to embark on a new workout programme, to get myself a new suit of armour – made of muscles.

Traditionally, English gentlemen are said to pay a lot of attention to their suits. To have one made at a tailor's in Savile Row would, I'm told, take more than a month. Well, it took far longer than that for me to develop a Premier League-quality suit of armour in collaboration with specialists at the club, including physios, a sports scientist and a nutritionist.

The process involved weight training, eating and resting, and it's not effective unless you take in sufficient nutrients, even if you work out regularly. There may even be a negative effect if your body can't recover properly due to lack of sleep. So getting the right balance between training, eating and sleeping is essential.

In principle, I hit the gym three days a week. Let's just suppose we had a game on Saturday (although nowadays there are Premier League matches on Monday and Friday evenings as well as on Sundays). A Saturday game would make Sunday a 'recovery day' for the team. But, for those who weren't involved in the game the day before, it would be a normal training day. If I was one of those I would do my weight training, let's say, focusing on my upper body, after the team training session on Sunday. Monday is normally a day off, and it's a day to rest my body, too. I'd be back in the gym on Tuesday, working on my lower body this time, and do another weight training focusing on my upper body on Thursday after a day's interval. Then, the same cycle starts again on the following Saturday. I take pride in having spent more time in the gym than any of my team-mates ever since I started doing this programme.

While I was engaged in the programme, there were moments when I felt a little dispirited, because not only was I still unable to win back my starting place but I was overtaken by team-mates who were recovering from injuries after showing positive results from their weight training. Those were times when I clearly felt the disadvantage of being a Japanese in the Western world.

Unfair DNA

There is an obvious difference in quantity and quality of muscles between Eastern and Western people. In my case, the end result of my regular weight training didn't become apparent any time soon after I started. Instead, my body changed very gradually over a long period. My wife, who was with me at home every day but had not seen me in the gym, didn't notice the change in my physique for quite a long time. Meanwhile, my European team-mates became visibly more muscular after making concentrated efforts in the gym for barely a month on their way to regaining full fitness. I was so jealous of the Western DNA! Virgil's physique, for instance, looked almost illegal to me, going totally against the law of oriental DNA. I'd never seen him doing anything particularly extra in the gym while he was at Southampton, but he always had what seemed to be an ideal body for a modern-day footballer, an athlete-cum-fighter on the pitch.

Fraser Forster, who also joined Southampton from Celtic but a year earlier than Virgil in the summer of 2014, is a goalkeeping giant whose huge frame seems completely beyond the Japanese standard to me. His arms are like those of a heavyweight boxer and just as powerful as their size suggests.

A goalkeeper usually tries to make himself look big, but Fraser could make the goal behind him look smaller at the same time by spreading his arms in front of an opponent about to shoot. When Fraser does that, making his already big body seem even bigger, I can understand why he has been called 'a great wall' by some in the British media. If he was a Japanese goalkeeper, he would have been called *Nurikabe*, after one of the monster characters from an old Japanese *manga*, *GeGeGe no Kitaro*, who is three metres tall and weighs a ton.

When a shot from close range hits an Asian goalkeeper's arm, the ball most likely pushes his arm backwards and continues its flight towards the goal, even if it ends up off target. But in the case of a big Premier League goalkeeper such as Fraser, he can push the ball back in the opposite direction with his powerful arms and hands. Whether it's the size of one's frame or one's muscle mass and the power it contains, there's no denying the inherent physical differences.

But then again, there is no point crying for the moon. Instead, we should focus on our own advantages. In my case, I could be a better defender with my mobility and ability to turn more quickly and sharply than bulkier defenders in the Premier League. Compared to someone with both power and speed, I may be more supple in my movements. However, I still needed to bring my physical strength up to the Premier League average. And I had to do whatever it took to achieve that. If my competitors have three times more muscle, I told myself I should spend three times longer in the gym. That was the determination I had as I approached the programme to improve my physical strength.

Mundane but long, or short but exciting

My attitude was the same when I was in the club's canteen located on the floor above our dressing room. For a gourmet samurai from a land of rich food culture, it would have been ideal if I could reward my hard work on the training ground and in the gym with a delicious lunch. However, to maximise the effect of my weight training, I had a plate of chicken breast day after day. I shoved those fillets – low in fat but bland in taste – down my throat, merely as a source of protein needed for muscle growth. It was as though I were in the canteen for the nutrient intake alone rather than for lunch.

I also started taking supplements after consulting with the club's nutritionist. Taking amino acid supplements while you are trying to build up your muscle mass is a common practice even in Japan, although I think the knowledge and use of supplements is not as advanced as in the United States or in Europe.

I had read an article somewhere that said some American athletes had instead started taking HMB (beta-Hydroxy beta-methylbutyric acid), a metabolite of the essential amino acid, as a more effective supplement since HMB, rather than the essential amino acid on its own, had now been thought to help prevent muscle breakdown. When I asked for more information and some advice, our nutritionist explained to me in detail about the supplement, which might have a side effect if too much was taken but would be almost useless if taken in insufficient quantities.

At a Premier League club, players are supported by many specialists in the first-team staff. For example, we have separate physiotherapists, one for exercise and one for rehabilitation. At that time, Southampton shared a nutritionist with the England national rugby team and he came down to Staplewood every other week to check players' body fat. So I could easily ask for an expert's opinion about the effective use of dietary supplements.

Taking supplements in general may be the norm for modern-day athletes, including footballers. But for me it was something new. It was certainly a change; I had intentionally avoided touching supplements until then.

I used to believe that I should not put anything unnatural into my body if I wanted to prolong my playing career. Supplements to me represented something chemical, akin to painkillers that I worried would cause some serious damage to my body by the age of 30 or so if taken too frequently. But my attitude changed while I was struggling to get enough playing time. Somewhere during that long period of darkness I started thinking about which sounds more successful to me: a career that lasts until the age of 40 at an average level or a career that ends at the age of 30 at the top level. I found myself choosing the latter.

The definition of a successful career depends on each person's perspective. There's no right or wrong, or better or worse. To prolong a playing career, one has to keep sacrificing part of your private life by staying on a strict diet, for instance. My sincere respect goes to my fellow professionals, who maintain their hunger and dedication even as they get older and the end of their careers comes nearer.

My perspective had shifted more towards 'How high is the level I can reach?' and 'What could I achieve at a higher level?' than 'How many years can I carry on playing?' as far as my own career was concerned. I had become a player who would feel more satisfied if I was seen as real Premier League class, although finished at 30, bowing out soon after becoming a seasoned professional. Taking supplements was one of the decisions I therefore took.

I even changed my diet further. I tried to stay away from rice, part of my staple diet as a Japanese, since I had heard a rice-free diet would make me feel more energetic. I usually take my breakfast and lunch at the club, so a Japanese evening meal prepared by my wife at home is always something I look forward to. But I sacrificed that personal pleasure when I started my muscle-building programme.

However, the 'no rice' diet only lasted for about two months. I was meant to feel a difference after one month but it didn't seem to be the case for me. In the end, I thought it would suit me better to enjoy my evening meal with rice, and work even harder in the gym to burn the extra carbohydrates from the rice inside my body, instead of continuing with my new diet and feeling frustrated about not having rice at all in my day's diet.

It took about three or four months for me to start feeling some positive effect from the programme. Finally, in the months afterwards, others started to notice the change in my body, saying things like, 'Your chest looks much thicker.' My new suit of armour was the result of long and hard work, at a cost of lots of sweat and occasional tears.

Power, speed and dark arts

It would be a bit like putting the cart before the horse if my new armour of muscles ended up slowing me down as a player, as all my body-building efforts had been aimed at making my mobility and agility count as real strengths as a Premier League centre-back.

I don't think I'm particularly quick among Japanese players but I must be faster than a typical strongly built Premier League centre-back. I've always felt more than capable of covering space and making interceptions, and I wanted to use that aspect of my play to make me a better-than-average Premier League centre-back.

Therefore, in addition to the extra work I was doing at the club, I had continued my individual training sessions with Tatsuo Sugimoto, my privately hired sprint coach from my time in the Netherlands. I could say I even put more emphasis on my sprint training.

We had started working on the movement of my legs long before I embarked on the programme. Even a simple exercise, which just seems like walking with an exaggerated knee lift, is an effective workout for muscles usually in use only when making a sprint. Over time, this exercise helps give you a quicker start and more acceleration.

We added a workout to improve the use of my arms in our training menu in my second year at VVV-Venlo, i.e.

a year before my arrival at Southampton. It meant I started hitting the gym with a proper plan in my fifth year, since I had already started working on the movements of my arms in sprinting. While I was trying to gain more muscle mass in my upper body, I could put extra focus on sessions with my sprint coach in order to make sure that my weight training would not make my running slower.

My sprint training sessions are completely separate from my training at the club. In my early days at Southampton, when I still didn't know much about the local sports facilities, we sometimes had our sessions on the common near where I used to live. When I was recovering from my knee ligament (MCL) injury, which prevented me from doing proper sprinting exercises, Sugimoto-san still gave me a training menu that I could follow at home. Since he is also a personal trainer for Ryo Miyaichi, who joined Arsenal in 2011 but left for FC St Pauli in Germany in 2015 following a series of loan moves, I even went to Hamburg on one occasion to join in their training session, using my rare two days off during the season.

To me, hiring a personal trainer is part of my self-investment as a professional player. I think that it is a player's own responsibility to protect and maintain his competitiveness in the team and to be recognised as a force. By executing my plan to improve my physical strength while carrying on doing my personal sprint training, I realised that I could be more than a match for my Premier League opponents. Even though I'm still only of average physical strength in terms of Premier League defenders, I now have more chance to get to the ball before my opponent thanks to my improved start and acceleration. If I get to the ball first, it doesn't really matter if my opponent fits in my 'physical monster' category, as I can win the ball without a physical clash. I can honestly say that there are now more cases in which I get to the ball more quickly than my opponent as a result of my continued sprint training.

Needless to say, there are still occasions when I find myself in a fifty-fifty situation on the pitch, but even then I no longer feel that the odds are stacked against me. If it's fifty-fifty to get to the ball first, it is also a fifty-fifty chance for me or the other player to come out on top afterwards. There are still players such as Romelu Lukaku of Manchester United or Christian Benteke of Crystal Palace, who make you feel as if you are smashing into a huge rock when you charge at them, but I can now at least compete with them with my full might. They won't flinch, either, so it may look as though we are casually body-checking each other, but the fact is that I'm charging at my opponent with full force. If I played like that against a Japanese player, he would easily be shoved to the floor and I'd probably be penalised for a foul. But I have to charge that hard against a Premier League opponent when competing for the ball. Were such a scene to be depicted in a *manga* comic strip, the accompanying onomatopoeia should read 'BOOM!' rather than 'BANG!'

In the Premier League, the phrase 'dark arts' is used about a defender sometimes, meaning he commits a foul to stop his opponent without being spotted by a referee. Shortly after my Southampton début I was surprised by the fact that the elbows I received from attacking players I was marking were not deemed illegal, but I also became aware that defenders, too, would use every trick in the book to stop the opposition scoring, especially in set-play situations. Some would hold the other team's striker in a way I can only describe as putting him in a headlock.

I don't think I'm a practitioner of the defensive dark arts, and I don't want to be one, either. For a defender, I've received relatively few cautions and, as a samurai on the football pitch, I shall stick with my ideals – that is, to win a battle fair and square without using underhand tricks. First, I try to get to the ball first. If I can't, then I try to prevent my opponent with the ball from turning towards the goal. If he turns and faces the goal, I try to stop him from advancing. And if that fails, too, I might have to foul him as the very last resort for the team. I don't want to change this order in my choices. The principle remained unchanged even after I improved my physique and became more competitive in grappling battles in the box when I had to participate in them.

Elusive man of the match

In the West Ham game, which I chose as the key match in my fourth season at Southampton, we picked up three points with a clean sheet as a team, and I personally gained some hope first, and then had quite a shock to fuel my resolve to work my way out to exit from the darkness. But there was one thing I still couldn't pick up on that day – a man of the match trophy. It used to be a magnum bottle of champagne when I joined Southampton, and the current design resembles a metallic gold brick. In the 2015/16 season it was a trophy with a ball-shaped top.

It's not that I wanted the trophy itself, but I wanted the accolade of being recognised as the man of the match. I felt, after that West Ham game, that my defensive display had been at least on a par with that of my fellow defenders, and it was I who had also scored the winning goal.

However, the man of the match accolade went to Virgil, who played in the middle of our back three. Don't get me wrong. He played well too. But I couldn't help but feel a bit disappointed, knowing that even a game-winning performance wasn't enough for me to be considered as a recipient. 'Is it because I'm an Asian player?' The thought occurred to me for just a moment.

During the season, I also felt that my compatriot and Leicester City striker Oka-chan (Shinji Okazaki) wasn't really getting the spotlight he deserved on the BBC's *Match of the Day* programme, despite the fact that he was one of the driving forces in their team achieving the miracle of becoming the 2015/16 Premier League champions. Occasionally, it seemed, a Japanese player would be mentioned on the programme, but rarely so. I began to develop a sort of victim complex, and even thought that it was another hurdle for me to clear as a Japanese player in the Premier League.

In reality, the reason for me not being awarded a man of the match trophy or featured on *Match of the Day* was simply that I'm not good enough, not because I'm an Asian player. I would soon be made to realise that while still on my way out from the darkness.

A week after the West Ham game, I spent the whole 90 minutes back on the bench at Swansea City's Liberty Stadium. It was a time when Koeman, our manager, was frequently making changes to the starting line-up. Cédric Soares, who played as a wing-back on the right-hand side in the previous game, was also sitting on the bench with me. Among our defenders, it was only the first choice centre-back pair of Virgil and José Fonte, and Ryan Bertrand, a left-back by trade but the player who replaced me on the left-hand side of our back three against Swansea, whose starting places were guaranteed bar injuries and suspensions. It seemed as though I had still not won the manager's trust to make him think, 'I should play him instead from now on,' regardless of whether it was four or three at the back.

All I could do was to show on the pitch the improvements I had made every time I was given a chance to play. If I could prove to my manager that I was a proper Premier League defender, recognition by the media would follow regardless of my nationality. I changed my thinking to adopt that view.

At the same time, my attitude towards myself as a Japanese player went through a change as well.

When I first arrived in England, I saw myself representing my countrymen by taking up a challenge in the Premier League. I felt that I came here to fight on behalf of other Asian defenders. Just as a samurai in the old days went to the headquarters of another clan to issue a challenge, wanting to bring its members to their knees, I came here to prove my skills against the masters in the home of football. And I felt I had a responsibility, by becoming a mainstay at Southampton, to make inroads for my fellow footballers in Asia to try their luck in the Premier League.

But as time went by I came to see that such a way of thinking might confine me to being Japanese while I was actually in a global environment in the Premier League. I realised I saw myself too much as a *Japanese* defender, and that it would not be enough to gain a reputation as 'good for a Japanese' or 'a top Asian defender' if I wanted to be truly recognised in the Premier League. My sense of purpose thus changed at some point during my time at Southampton from 'succeed as an Asian for other Asian players' to 'succeed as a Premier League player'.

As a human being, my pride in being Japanese has never changed. But as a footballer, I want to be recognised not as a Japanese centre-back named Maya Yoshida, but as Maya Yoshida the Premier League centre-back. Some day I want people to see me and simply say, 'Maya is a good defender,' as opposed to 'Maya is a good Japanese defender.' That has become one of my tangible goals since around the year 2016.

Headband and free kick

Off the pitch, I also made an intentional change. I had an urge to change my hairstyle. The idea came to me when I was casually reading a Japanese magazine called *Sports Graphic Number* that I received as a sample copy at Staplewood one day. On one page there was a team photo of the Japan national team. It was one of those typical pre-match team photos in which the players line up in two rows, with the boys in the front squatting on their heels.

Some of my Southampton team-mates came round to take a look at the photo and went, 'Where's Maya?' They see me almost every day but couldn't spot me in the photo right away. Not only that, they said to me, 'You all have the same haircut.' To my mind, I look very different from someone like Hasebe-san (Makoto Hasebe), our national team captain who plays for Eintracht Frankfurt, even though we both sported a short hairstyle back then. We look totally different. But according to my English and European team-mates we all looked the same.

Then I remembered when we played against Scandinavian countries I'd felt that all their players, each with white skin and blond hair, looked very similar to each other. I had never thought that the opposite might apply, but now I knew that we Japanese players, too, all look alike in European people's eyes.

I had been aware that I sometimes drew stares as a foreigner from people abroad. It was certainly the case when I was living in Venlo, where there weren't many Asians around; very few Chinese, let alone Japanese. But the thought didn't really occur to me that we might all look the same to them. Now it did. So I decided to change my hairstyle.

Identity is very important. I can't be just the same as all others. On the other hand, having short hair to start with, I didn't have many choices for my new style. In the end I chose the one commonly known as 'two-block', after taking my hair type and the shape of my face into account. I also decided on that look because, at that time, there weren't too many players sporting the same hairstyle in Europe.

I always have my hair cut by a Japanese hairdresser who works in a hair salon in Covent Garden in London. When I was playing for VVV, I was a regular customer at a Japanese hairdresser's in Düsseldorf after getting what I felt was a disastrously uneven haircut at a local hairdresser in the Netherlands. Japanese hair is generally much thicker than Europeans' and can be unfamiliar to Western hairdressers. So, if styled by a European hairdresser, a rather unwelcome surprise can be in store for us Japanese more often than not. My preference for a native Japanese hairdresser may never change, no matter how close I get to becoming a true cosmopolitan.

Nowadays, the 'two-block' has become quite popular among players in England. It may be about time for me to change my hairstyle again soon!

Talking about hairstyles, what is called a 'centre-part', with a rubber headband over longish hair, was the popular choice among J.League players when I was promoted to the first team at Nagoya Grampus Eight. I never went for that style myself. I think I can hear some of you readers saying, 'You'll look awful with that hairstyle!' But that point aside, I've never been one to follow a trend just because it is fashionable (although if my Southampton team-mates see a Grampus team photo from that era, they might still say, 'You all have the same hairstyle,' as I had my hair a little longer than it is today).

My motivation behind putting in long hours on improving my dead-ball skill likewise stemmed from a desire to go against fixed opinions. When I was at school, I didn't want others to say, 'He lacks manners because he left home young,' or 'He can't get a decent grade because he only plays football.' From a young age I simply couldn't accept fixed ideas or stereotypical views about myself. In a way, that attitude has helped push me to prove wrong those who said things like, 'He won't make it as a professional because he's a boy from the small town of Nagasaki,' or 'He can't cut it overseas because he's a Japanese centre-back.'

Similarly, I was determined to go against the view that 'He's a centre-back, so he can only defend.' As part of my efforts to overturn that stereotype, I started to practise free kicks after a team training session some time before the 2014 World Cup. At that time, Yatto-san (Yasuhito Endo) seemed more or less the only player we could call on in the Japan national team when the situation asked for a right-footed kicker. So I thought I could at least have a chance to be an alternative kicker if I could improve my free-kick ability through practice.

In general, centre-backs are not known for their skill but for their toughness. It's the same in Japan or in England. People usually see a centre-back as a player who is on the pitch to defend. Unsurprisingly, then, my team-mates used to crack jokes as soon as I started practising free kicks after the team training sessions. In the national team they mocked me, saying, 'Maya, what the hell are you doing?', while my teammates at Southampton shouted, 'Seriously Maya, stop fooling around!' or made similar comments.

However, my immunity from ridicule, a part of my resilience developed over some 20 years of my life, is not to be ignored. Having practised free kicks on my own throughout two seasons with my team-mates laughing and chuckling in the background, I have managed to put my name onto the list of free-kick takers in the team.

At first, some of my team-mates still joked, saying, 'Why are you on the list?', but these days they sometimes even say, 'You should take one,' when we are awarded a free kick during the game.

I usually reply, 'I do fancy one,' but I also know I'm still not at the top of the list. At Southampton, Prowsey (James Ward-Prowse) is the team's first-choice kicker. Next time we get a free kick, if he happens not to be on the pitch I would love to take it and score.

Just as it was only after I broke my Premier League duck with a headed goal in my second year at Southampton that my team-mates started to see me as one of the key target men in an offensive set-piece situation, so I have to keep on trying to show some end product to disprove the notion that 'He can only defend because he's a centre-back.' To this day, every week I have been practising my free kicks after training sessions.

My *ideal centre-back*

Quite apart from the change in my hairstyle, whether it concerned my physical strength or my free kicks, people said some nice things about my efforts once I started to show signs of improvement on the pitch. It made me feel rather good. But at the same time, I knew that I shouldn't expect people to recognise and praise the effort I had made, because it was merely something I did while trying to produce a result. That is the way I see it.

In the world of professional footballers, the result is what matters. With a tangible result, then the process leading up to it can be appreciated. Without a result, the whole process is just something done in the past.

Everything I thought I was doing extra at the beginning, be it the weight training in the gym, the nutritional care including supplements, or sprint training with my personal trainer, was just a part of the necessary process as a professional footballer. It was merely a business effort, as if I were a one-man corporation. And its success is all down to my actual sales activity; that is, my performance on the pitch to increase my sales figures by bringing home the maximum three points for the team in as many matches as possible.

Even when I initially felt I saw a tiny light at the end of the tunnel, and then became more constructively determined not to succumb to the ensuing despair and to head towards the exit in the second half of the 2015/16 season, I was still in the process of making a mere business effort. It was nothing extra or special, but was something fundamental, which I had to do continually as a professional.

One of those tasks is reviewing my performance in a match. I've always been a calm and keen observer ever since I was little, but the person I should look at with my keenest eye is myself as a player on the pitch. I have watched afterwards every game in which I played to review my performance since the time I was a youth-team player at Grampus.

At Southampton we can watch the footage on a tablet on the day after our day off following the match. There are two choices. One is a 20-minute-long piece of footage consisting almost entirely of scenes of each player's touches of the ball, and the other is a full 90-minute recording of the game. I always go for the 90-minute version because I don't think I can really judge whether my decision-making or ball touch was good or bad unless I see what was going on before and after that moment. This point of view is also one I've had since my youth-player days. I review my performance in each game and identify my faults, which I then aim to rectify, and points I can improve on. I have been doing that for over 10 years now.

One of the things I picked up about myself by reviewing my performances as a Southampton player was how frequently I made safety the first priority when I was really struggling to get opportunities in the team. It's not a bad attitude to have for a defender in principle. In and around our own penalty area, there are times when it's right for a defender to play with safety-first in mind rather than trying to do something more complicated and end up losing the ball to invite danger. But back then, when I was given the rare opportunity to start or come off the bench, I was thinking too much about playing safe and simple, I have to admit.

Being too conscious about safety-first makes you no more than an average defender, one who can only get 6 or 6.5 out of 10 marks at the maximum. That's not a bad mark for someone playing regularly, but I needed to make my case on the pitch to win a regular starting place. Not only that, if I want to be recognised as a top-class player I should be able to perform constantly at a 7 or 8 out of 10 level. I believe that we gain more courage by overcoming difficulties or dangers in a battle one by one, but being desperate to be on the pitch, which is a battle-field for footballers, I forgot the essence of what a warrior is at that time.

Under normal circumstances, a more courageous approach, such as breaking from the line to cover the space or initiating an attack from the back line, are my fortes. Repelling a cross with a strong header or blocking a shot by throwing your body in the way are examples of 'toughness' in a centre-back; giving directions to defensive team-mates, reading the game, on the other hand, reacting quicker than anyone to intercept an opponent's pass and then feeding the ball to a team-mate, represent 'subtleness' – another important facet of a centre-back. And I had come to realise that I would need to show these two facets on Premier League pitches in order for me to be recognised.

I had already started working diligently according to my physical training programme. Meanwhile, the football intelligence needed for the 'subtleness' side of play is one thing that I have always regarded as the most important quality for a centre-back. It was Piksi (Dragan Stojković), the manager of Grampus when I decided to play in Europe aged 21, who told me, 'What is most important for a defender is his intelligence.'

Those words have never left my mind no matter how hard the physical battle is or how high emotions are running on the pitch. A defender must always stay cool-headed and calm.

In a Premier League match it can be a mad world, especially inside the box. In a set-piece situation it can feel like being in a packed commuter train in Japan, apart from the fact that the box is full of men over six feet tall. Even in open play, you might face wave after wave of attack following a rapid counter-move, especially since more teams have started to attack in numbers with a possession-based style of football in recent seasons.

That's why being cool-headed is very important for a defender. In some situations you need to make a decision to abandon your marking duty momentarily and close down the player on the ball or cover space that is at risk of being occupied by an opponent. This ability to make quick decisions has become even more significant as more and more teams in the Premier League adopt a style of pressing football. This style requires a higher defensive line than before, leaving more space behind the back line, and so demands a centre-back to sharpen up his sense of awareness and ability not only to put the opponent in front under pressure but also to be able to cover the space behind.

If I can cover more space in the defensive third of the pitch, it will enable my team-mates to go forward to attack more. Our full-backs, who are my defensive colleagues but are also tasked with attacking as well, can benefit from my positioning, as their energy-sapping workload is reduced if they can take a higher starting position.

Both at Southampton and with the Japan national team, I want to be a centre-back who makes our full-backs feel, 'I can go forward without worrying too much, knowing that Maya can cover the space behind.' I also want our central midfielders in front of me to think, 'I can try to win back the ball higher up the pitch as Maya will move up from the back to fill the space.' And, of course, I want to stop the opponent's attacks by reading the game intelligently, or by being physically strong, and to deliver forward passes to my team-mates when I see a chance.

I want to be a centre-back equipped with both tough-ness and subtlety at a high Premier League standard. The image of my ideal centre-back had gradually become clearer in my head while I was struggling and searching for my way out from the darkness. Also, I had become more aware that I was in an ideal environment to improve both the 'toughness' and 'subtleness' sides of my play as a centre-back.

Knowing that, I can now calmly say that those times of tribulation were meaningful and important for me in my football career: my second year at Southampton, in which the pitch seemed further away than I had ever felt before and I was struggling desperately in the tunnel; my third year, which was spent still in the darkness; and the fourth year, where I had another false dawn but what I would need to do to get out and what kind of centre-back I would want to be after exiting the tunnel became clear to me.

CHAPTER 6

SAMURAI RESILIENCE

Another new beginning

The player-profile page on Southampton's official website at the beginning of the 2016/17 season had me down as '189 cm (6' 2"), 78 kg (172 lbs)'. In reality, my weight had increased to 86 kg (190 lbs) while there was no change in my height, as you would expect of someone already in his late twenties. My weight gain was not down to vast quantities of fish and chips, which I believe every tourist should try at least once when visiting the United Kingdom, but thanks to my weight training. Just as my body had gone through a positive transformation, the fifth year since my arrival turned out to be a year of positive changes for me.

Following an almost customary managerial change during the summer, two starting places for centre-backs that had more or less belonged to Virgil van Dijk and José Fonte until the end of the previous season became available once again for all to win under a new manager. It was rather welcome for me.

Ronald Koeman, our previous manager, had gone to Everton after guiding Southampton to a top-six finish in

his second year in the Premier League. His successor was
Claude Puel. I don't think people in England knew much
about the French manager from Nice, apart from the fact
that he once played under Arsène Wenger at Monaco as
a defensive midfielder.

He looked serious. A bit scary, even. That was my first
impression of him, although I soon realised that I was
wrong. It was only because his slight shyness combined
with his struggles with the English language when he first
arrived at Southampton projected an image of a somewhat distant man. Once I had a chance to chat with him,
I understood he was in fact a very nice man. As a manager,
too, he trusted me and took me into his squad-rotation
system.

When you hear the word 'rotation', you may automatically think about the second half of the season and the
usual fixture congestion from the festive period onwards.
But in the 2016/17 season Southampton also had games
in the League Cup and in Europe from the second month
of the season.

As of now, a maximum of seven English clubs can
qualify to play in the UEFA competitions. In the
Champions League the top three clubs in the Premier
League qualify for the group stage, while the fourth-
placed club in the final league table qualifies for the play-
off round. Also, the fifth-placed Premier League club

qualifies for the group stages in the Europa League, as do the winners of the FA Cup. The League Cup winners qualify for its third qualifying round.

Southampton had finished the 2015/16 season sixth in the Premier League but still qualified for the Europa League because fifth-placed Manchester United won the FA Cup. Although our European adventure ended early in the group stage, after we missed out on one of the top two spots in our group needed to go through to the knockout stage, I played the full 90 minutes in all of the six group games, with Virgil as my centre-back partner.

Meanwhile, I partnered José in the middle of our back line in the League Cup from the third round onwards. From the outside I might still have looked unable to win back my regular starting place, much as in the previous three years, but I personally felt that the situation surrounding me in the team was changing. I knew that I was in a better place both physically and mentally, too. I felt confident that, this time, I was finally ready to be a regular starter again in the Premier League once I started getting opportunities in the other competitions.

Maya the speedster

There was also a pleasantly surprising change regarding myself in my fifth year as a Southampton player. I managed to reverse the clichéd image of the lumbering centre-back thanks to a story in the *Daily Mirror*.

In October 2016 the newspaper revealed my deceptively quick running ability to the public as one of 'seven shock discoveries' in the Premier League. The article was accompanied by a photo of me looking somewhat zany on the pitch, with a caption saying 'Not even Maya believes that one.' The reason for my inclusion was that my sprinting speed had been recorded in the season at 34.78 km/h – exactly the same as Theo Walcott's.

If you ask me if I'm a quick or slow runner, my answer would be 'somewhere between average and fast'. I'm probably only around the sixth or seventh quickest among my Southampton team-mates. Longy (Shane Long) is the fastest, with Virgil 'the alien' in second place while he was with us, and then Ryan Bertrand, Charlie Austin, perhaps any one of the young players and me, in that order, I think.

Outside Southampton, players such as Sadio Mané of Liverpool, Eden Hazard of Chelsea and Raheem Sterling of Manchester City are all 'speed monsters', according to my own categorisation. If I would describe them as cheetahs, arguably the fastest animal on earth, I would perhaps call myself a zebra (my stripes being the red-and-white ones of Southampton).

Having said that, I knew I wasn't one of the slower players in the team even before the story in the newspaper. As we train with a GPS device, we are all aware of the data. My top speed was only about 0.5 km/h slower than Longy, so my team-mates likewise believed I was relatively quick.

But outside Southampton, especially back in Japan, people had thought differently. Uchiy (Atsuto Uchida) once called me 'slow-footed', as simple as that, and even described my sprint as 'jogging' when he kindly agreed to appear in one of my previous books published in Japan.

People in Japan got to know about the English newspaper article through various channels online and began to talk about the revelation that 'Yoshida is as quick as Walcott.' The lumbering centre-back image that had been associated with me for such a long time was erased in an instant. Needless to say, my trusted sprint coach, Sugimoto-san, and I were both delighted. I was punching the air in my mind, and so was he, I believe.

The most precious change

In England, late November makes me feel that I'm already in the chill winter, in contrast to that end-of-the-autumn feeling I have at the same time of year when I'm in Japan. But in November 2016 I experienced the happiest and warmest change in my life so far. I became a father, my baby daughter being born at the Royal Hampshire County Hospital in Winchester where I live.

Once again, I have Miku to thank for being able to hold our baby in my arms, the day she came into this world here in England. At first, my wife was going to go back to Japan to give birth. I have heard that returning home is quite common among Japanese women living abroad because it gives them more of a sense of security being back in their native country where they don't have to worry about the language, as well as a lack of family support, especially from their parents.

But with the baby due around the end of November, it meant that if my wife was going to give birth in Japan I wouldn't be able to see her or my child until the following spring, when I would be returning to join the national team. I couldn't expect her to bring a newborn baby on a 12-hour flight to the United Kingdom. Moreover, the team schedule comes first while I'm on national team duty, and I wouldn't have had much time to spend with my wife and baby even if I'd been there in Japan. So, in reality, I would have to wait until the off-season to be with my family properly, by which time our baby would have been six months old. I felt that would be too long and very sad for me, and so had to ask my understanding wife to grant my selfish wish.

Day after day I begged her to stay, saying such things as, 'I don't think there are many Japanese women who have a chance to give birth in the United Kingdom.' 'It's cool to give birth here, isn't it?' Or, 'I guarantee you my full support!' In the end, not because of my successful attempts to entice her, but purely because of the warm-heartedness of my wife, we decided to welcome our baby into our lives right here. As both a husband and a father, I owe so much to my wife for her kindness and courage.

It was 19 November, the day of the Liverpool game at home, when Miku's waters broke, at around three in the morning, I think. I called a midwife straight away but was told to wait upon her visit. She came round again later in the morning to check my wife but her advice was the same – 'Not yet.' Getting a little anxious, I also called the hospital just in case, but once more I was told to wait at home, to the surprise of this novice father-to-be.

At the time, I thought I would wait at home with my wife, as I already knew I wouldn't be starting the game. I then called Hugo, our players' liaison officer, and asked him to check if it would be OK with the manager to miss the match. The answer was, 'He still wants you to be available on the bench for now,' although I was given permission to leave for the hospital at any point during the game if my wife went into labour, as it is almost mandatory for a husband in Britain to attend the birth of his baby nowadays.

Usually, we players are supposed to leave our mobile phones in the dressing room, but on that particular day I took mine with me and handed it to Hugo, who sits behind our bench at St Mary's Stadium. During the game I was of course watching what was happening on the pitch in front of me, but every time the play stopped I couldn't help but look behind me and have a little exchange with Hugo along the lines of, 'Not yet?' – 'No,' or 'So?' – 'Still no sign,' with our eyes. The game ended as a goalless draw, and there was no baby for the Yoshidas, either, on that day.

We spent one more night at home and went to the hospital together the following morning, as it had been explained to us beforehand that there would be a small risk of bacterial infection for the baby after 24 hours of my wife's waters breaking. Fortunately, it was only a five-minute drive away. But even after my wife was taken to a bed in the maternity unit, there was still no sign of the baby arriving any time soon. Miku kept battling labour pains right through to midnight and beyond. She was in a battle way tougher and longer than a football game going into extra time and then to a penalty shoot-out. Yet, all I could do was just be beside her and watch her in pain. That made me so frustrated, with so many emotions; appreciation, encouragement and concern for her, all came flooding inside me.

Then, the moment finally arrived. The moment when we became parents. I just wanted our baby to be born healthy. I didn't mind what she would call me when she grew up – 'otosan' (dad in Japanese), 'daddy', 'papa' or whatever. But there was one thing I secretly wished for our baby. I wanted her to have double eyelids above her charming eyes (by the way, I'm the only one with single eyelids among the five members of the Yoshida family in Nagasaki). When I saw my baby daughter for the first time at the hospital, my wife said to me, 'She has double eyelids,' before anything else. I felt tears trickling down my face on my 'dad début' in England.

I owe heartfelt thanks to Miku for agreeing to give birth overseas despite her initial anxiety. If I could be allowed to be selfish one last time and ask one more thing of her, it would be that she will tell our daughter the story of my 'great proposal' one day. After listening to the full story – including how I completely surprised my wife-to-be and touched her heart when I proposed to her in a tuxedo on the hill where we had our first kiss – my daughter would surely think, 'I want someone equally in love with me and even more romantic than my dad when I get married!' (Oh no, no! It's way too early. I don't even want to think about the day my daughter gets married yet!)

When I proposed to Miku, I gave her an 'engagement watch', one of a pair of his-and-her watches I bought for the special occasion, instead of an engagement ring. With her, I have experienced a wonderful passage of life ever since we started seeing each other when we were in Japan.

Our first step together as parents was a hugely meaningful experience for both of us, to the extent that even I, who wasn't the one who actually gave birth, became tougher as a human being simply through going through it all with my wife.

The process of pregnancy and birth also enhanced my English vocabulary. Previously, it was limited to words and expressions related to my football and day-to-day life, but my wife's pregnancy exposed me to a new set of words that I had never even heard of before, such as 'obstetrician' and 'gynaecologist' to start with.

One of the advantages of being a professional footballer is that we have shorter working hours compared to office-goers. On a normal training day I can be home by three or four in the afternoon. By switching between football and babysitting, i.e. focusing and unwinding, I feel my days have become even more fulfilling on and off the pitch since becoming a father. When I'm home I always bathe my baby daughter. It's also me who tucks her up, and by falling asleep myself with her around nine in the evening I'm getting more than enough sleep, too.

Curiously enough, it was when I had this most precious moment in my life towards the halfway point of the season that I began to experience the joy of playing regular football again at Southampton. In my mind, the birth of my baby daughter and my resurrection from the darkness overlap peculiarly.

Miku has given me the best present a man could possibly ask for, and my baby daughter Ema has brought me luck upon her birth. Here, I want to say from the bottom of my heart, and in bold letters, to the two female members of my family, 'I LOVE YOU.'

Big game

On 26 February 2017 at Wembley Stadium under a clouded sky, I took part in 'the' game which I had been so looking forward to for a month since we made it to the final at this magnificent stadium.

In the 2016/17 season I started and played the full 90 minutes in 37 games in total, meaning I managed to spend more time on the pitch than in my first season at Southampton, in which I played a total of 34 games. Among those 37 games, this game against Manchester United in the League Cup final has to be the most memorable for me. It's also my choice for the key match in that season, the match where the new Maya Yoshida was born and answered some of his critics on the pitch.

Even though it is another cup competition, second to the FA Cup here in England, I really wanted to go all the way in the League Cup – called the EFL Cup in the 2016/17 season – partially because I was involved as a regular starter from its early rounds. If we won, it would also have been a significant achievement for the club in its fifth season back in the Premier League.

We were seen as underdogs in the final against United, who were going for their fifth triumph in the competition overall. Their manager, José Mourinho, in his first year at United, had previously won the competition three times as the Chelsea manager. Also, despite being stuck in sixth position in the league, United at that time were unbeaten in four league games prior to our clash in the final, showing some strong character – a mark of any Mourinho team.

On the other hand, we were coming into the final following two wins and four losses, and were eleventh in the table. For Southampton, with more than 130 years of history, the famous FA Cup victory in 1976 against United had remained the sole major title in the club's trophy cabinet, so another triumph was overdue.

We had reached Wembley despite our ill fortune in drawing Premier League opposition in each of the four rounds leading to the final. We beat Liverpool, the record eight-time League Cup winners, in the semi-finals. We were without José Fonte, who had handed in a transfer request before the first leg, and then lost Virgil to a long-term ankle injury before the second leg, but we still won each leg 1–0. We had won the previous three rounds with clean sheets as well. The team, including myself who played the 90 minutes in all of those five games, had gained confidence on the way to the final.

It was 23-year-old Jack Stephens who replaced the injured Virgil. He had been having a tough time, opportunities in the first team being almost non-existent for him. The game against Sunderland in the fourth round three months before the second leg of the semi-finals was only his second first-team appearance at Southampton. So the game at Anfield was the first big game he had ever tasted.

Like Jack, I also had a tough time in my early twenties, being sidelined for a long period at VVV-Venlo and sitting on the bench in so many games in my second year at Southampton. Therefore I could understand how frustrated he must have been. As someone who can relate to him, I always tried to encourage Jack, saying, 'Don't give up. Your chance will come if you keep working hard.' It was also my way of indirectly extra-motivating myself, since I knew that I would need to improve my performance, too, in order to win back my starting place properly.

I believe we also shared a desire to overcome some sort of inferiority complex. We both wanted to prove the people wrong who saw us as mere back-up options in the squad. This bond made it possible for us to form a strong centre-back partnership, not as a pair of senior and junior defenders, but as a unit in which we shared our views on equal terms and gave each other feedback after the game, once José left to join West Ham and Virgil fell victim to injury in the second half of the season.

This is Wembley

When we made it to the final, with Jack as my centre-back partner, by winning at Liverpool, who included two Brazil internationals in Philippe Coutinho and Roberto Firmino in their team, I was buzzing. I was too excited to go to bed that night.

On the day of the final, Wembley didn't disappoint me. The place was tingling with a big-game atmosphere. 'This must be the real Wembley,' I said to myself when I first stepped onto the pitch, excitement running through my body like an electric shock.

It wasn't my first time at Wembley, as I played there against Mexico in the semi-finals of the football tournament at the 2012 London Olympics. The stadium was filled with over 80,000 spectators for that game, too. But everything looked and felt different on the day of the League Cup final against United.

At the Olympic football game the atmosphere was more neutral. There were two sets of supporters in the stand, but to the British spectators the game between Mexico and Japan was an encounter between two foreign countries, which they couldn't be really passionate about. For the cup final, though, the stadium was split in two right down the middle, with each club's supporters occupying a half each. Listening to the deafening noise from the crowd, I seriously thought there were 30,000 to 40,000 more people in the stadium than at the Mexico game.

As a member of the Japan national Under-23 team at the time, I remember casually chatting to my team-mates, saying, 'I heard this is the sacred place for English football,' but on the day of my Wembley visit as a Southampton player I couldn't help but feel inspired, thinking, 'It's such a huge occasion to play in the final here at this stadium.' That League Cup final against United was the first *real* Wembley visit for me.

For that memorable occasion I arrived wearing a navy-coloured team suit with a pale blue shirt and a red tie. Our team coach pulled up right in front of the players' entrance to the stadium just before 3 p.m. Walking through the entrance and then turning left, there was the door to the dressing room area. The walls on the side of the door were decorated with the finalists' crest, United's on the left and ours on the right.

Once in our dressing room, carefully folded kit was tidily placed on the wooden but modern-looking bench for each player. Southampton had chosen to play in a white top and red shorts with a pair of white socks with red stripes at the top. We couldn't play in our home kit as red was the team colour of United, who were drawn as the home team for the final. Normally, we would then have played in our away kit, with black as the main colour. But as the game was such a special occasion for our supporters, most of whom were expected to come wearing our red-and-white striped home shirt on the day of our Wembley outing, the team had decided to play in our third-choice kit, whose colour combination at least was the same as our twelfth players in the stand.

As the 4 p.m. kick-off time drew near, I walked onto the pitch as the fourth player in our line after our captain Steven Davis, Fraser Forster and Orio (Oriol Romeu). As we came out from the players' tunnel I could see flame machines lined up on each side, a sheet in the shape and colour of each team's shirt placed on the pitch in front of us, and a giant crest-shaped balloon floating in the air above each half of the pitch. The final was about to kick off amid the huge roar and rapturous applause from the two sets of supporters – ours in the right half and United's in the left half of the stadium.

At the time, it was about four and a half years ago, also in north London, when I had made my Southampton début, shakily for a while after coming off the bench at the Emirates Stadium. But now I was feeling a tremor of excitement in our starting 11 in a big game at Wembley.

Winner's medal and loser's medal

For 90 minutes Southampton, the underdogs, were more than a match for United. I felt our overall performance was better than theirs. Our opening 'goal' early in the first half, scored by Manolo Gabbiadini who had just joined us from Napoli in the previous month, was disallowed for a marginal offside call, and then we conceded two goals in less than 30 minutes. Thankfully, Manolo put us right back in the game with two goals sandwiching half-time. It was us who then came close to getting the third goal first. I felt I was doing my job for the team individually, too, sliding in, for instance, to stop Jesse Lingard from pulling the trigger at a time when we were in the ascendancy and pushing to complete our comeback.

We were going head-to-head with United for victory … until three minutes from time when a firm close-range header by Zlatan Ibrahimovic mercilessly rippled the net in our goal. The Swedish striker, the biggest name among all the big names then at United, and now with LA Galaxy in the United States, had also opened the scoring for his team with a free kick from 30 yards out.

We had him under control for most of the 90 minutes, but couldn't prevent him from doing his job to make a difference in the end. The gutted feeling we had when he scored grew stronger as the time ticked away to the final whistle signalling our defeat. It was such a small difference on the pitch but it made a huge difference to the result. There were only three – plus four added on – minutes left before we could take the final to extra time, but one shot from Ibrahimovic, who found space between two defenders including myself inside the six-yard box, prevented that and won the title for United. Ultimately, it came down to how close we could get to closing the gap, a distance of a step and a half or so separating us at the real top level. I had improved myself, but on that day it wasn't quite enough. It's really about that at the end of the day. Always. People might think I'm saying the same thing all the time. But as you get to a higher level, the level of challenge in closing up the gap increases, too. That's the reality.

Real top players never miss an opportunity to take advantage of that small gap in quality to get a result. It was certainly the case with Ibrahimovic, who had become the main man at United soon after his move to Old Trafford in his mid-thirties. The same thing could be said about Mourinho, who had just won his first major title in his first year at United. People like these are treated as big names, and are regularly featured in the media even in the Far East and countries such as Japan, because they have repeatedly been winning battles at the top level, where a small margin makes a big difference. The accumulation of such victories is the foundation of their status. Ibrahimovic or Mourinho weren't born with a big-name tag or with the wealth and fame that comes along with it. They are what they are today only because they have honed their craft to be a winner at the top level through hard work and experience.

To be honest, I was thinking, 'He doesn't move around much,' when I was playing against Ibrahimovic in the

League Cup final. He didn't close us defenders down from the front line and didn't seem particularly keen to help his team-mates when defending. But he still did his main job well for the team – scoring goals. No matter how well Southampton took the game to United or how well we defended against them for the majority of the game – as people kindly point out that we did – the fact remains that Ibrahimovic took his two chances very well and United won the game as a result of his goals. He sometimes likens himself to a lion, to imply he is not a mere human being, but he is entitled to talk in such a confident way because he is a proven winner.

The game finished 3–2 to United. Some may see United as the cup winners and Southampton as the close runners-up. But the harsh reality is that, even though we were both finalists when the game kicked off, there was a clear distinction between United and us at the final whistle. United, who came out victorious after the 90 minutes, received what people here call a 'winner's medal' while we took a 'loser's medal' home. The clear difference in those phrases sums up the reality.

The post-match reaction not only from our own supporters who came to Wembley in their tens of thousands to cheer us on but also from the media was kind to a 'brave' Southampton left 'heartbroken'. Local Saints fans were still saying, 'It was a good game,' days after the final. But inside me I felt the sensation grow stronger day by day that having a good game is not enough.

Looking back now, I think our aim throughout the competition was simply to get to a Wembley final, whereas I believe United's players, such as Ibrahimovic, thought, 'This is what I came here for, to win'; they'd always imagined themselves winning the trophy at Wembley. That difference in our attitudes, I think, also contributed to our narrow defeat on the day. The higher the level, the little details matter more and a small gap in class makes an even bigger difference. It's nothing new to me, but it was still a painful experience. However, the valuable lesson taught by Ibrahimovic was the one thing I took from the League Cup final at Wembley from where, sadly, we couldn't bring the trophy home.

Twist of fate

Ibrahimovic and I go all the way back to when I was 15. I was still a youth-team player at Nagoya Grampus Eight when I saw him playing for Ajax in a game against Feyenoord when we travelled to the Netherlands. At that time I had no idea who Ibrahimovic was. Of course, I didn't know that he was already a Sweden international striker, either.

He came off the bench at one point in the game. He must have been still in his early twenties but he stood out nonetheless with his tall figure and the air of confidence he projected. I remember thinking, 'There's something different about him,' in the stand. Watching him play, I was impressed by his technique, and the way he touched the ball seemed kind of unique to me, too. That was my impression of this unknown player back then.

That indirect encounter with him was during the spring break before I entered high school in Japan. And after more than a decade I faced Ibrahimovic, who had become a very experienced world-class striker, on the pitch of the League Cup final as a defender at a Premier League club. 'This is unreal. Just like in the world of *manga*,' I felt. At Wembley I was moved by the wonder of a sport like football that can make such a thing happen in the real world, more than the fact that I had come a long way since I first saw him in the Netherlands.

In the *manga* called *Captain Tsubasa*, which I was an avid reader of when I was a kid, the lead character started from competing locally at elementary-school level, then stepped up to a national tournament where he would meet new rivals one after another, and, together with them, he would move on to the world stage, first at youth level and finally to the World Cup. I, similarly, left

Nagasaki for Nagoya when I finished elementary school, then progressed through the youth ranks to become a professional, and moved from Japan to Europe. Along the way, the level of games, competitions and my opponents became higher and higher, step by step. As a result, I had managed to reach the stage where I faced a foreign player, whom I watched from the stands when I was 15, in a big occasion at Wembley.

If my story as a footballer ever becomes a movie – let's call it 'Centre-back Maya' – I think it could inspire Japanese kids. It could be a vehicle to communicate the possibility and beauty of football as a sport through real-life events to the next generation.

If only I could have become living proof that dreams do come true by becoming a winner in the League Cup final in which I played against Ibrahimovic. I wanted to win the final so badly. Really.

100th Premier League appearance

It was around the end of April 2017 when I actually did something to inspire today's kids. I decided to invite 100 Japanese football kids to Southampton's home game against Hull City. Why 100 kids? It was because I was likely to reach my 100th appearance in the Premier League in that game.

Once I actually reached that number, I felt, 'Still only 100,' more than a sense of achievement. When people talk about the Premier League's 100 club, it's about the players who scored 100 goals or more in the league. There would be too many members if we formed another 100 club based on league appearances.

Having said that, 100 league appearances had been one of my personal goals to achieve. It was in my fourth year at Southampton when I set that target. I had privately arranged to see a sports psychologist in that year, thinking that it might help improve my mental strength, including my concentration levels on the pitch. In one of our sessions we came to the conclusion that it would be better for me to have a tangible individual target as a player, so I picked 100 Premier League appearances, as it seemed an achievable yet not too easy goal. I was genuinely pleased about the fact that I achieved the personal mark in the following year.

The kids I invited to the game were all from a private football school called Football Samurai Academy, based in west London. It is the largest Japanese football school in Europe, running from Under-7 up to Under-17 teams, together with a first team called London Samurai United which competes in the twelfth tier of the English football pyramid. I had got to know the academy owner some time ago and become friends with its coaches, who are more or less of my generation. In fact, I'm now a principal of the academy. I can't say that I'm busy doing anything in particular at the academy, as it's more of an honorary post. But yes, it's true that there is another side of me as 'headmaster Yoshida' in front of my samurai kids.

Most of the kids at the academy are from families of Japanese expatriates living in and around London. They can go and watch some Premier League games at weekends by themselves if they want to. However, I didn't think many of them had been to St Mary's, which is about one and a half hours away from London by train, and there seemed to be some who had never been to a football game despite living in the home of football.

So, when I was thinking about what I could do for the kids at the academy, I thought it would be good if I invited them to our game. I'm not sure if they had the same feeling in the stand on the day of the Hull game as I did all those years ago when I was 15, watching Ibrahimovic playing in the Netherlands. But at least they saw their fellow countryman playing in a Premier League match, and if that inspires even only one of them to think, 'I can do it if he can,' after watching me from the stand, I'll be very happy. On that day I wanted to send them the message that everybody has a chance.

After the game I managed to spend a little time with the samurai kids. I received a bouquet and nice messages from them congratulating me on my 100th league appearance. I took some pictures with the possible future Japanese Premier League players. I was thankful to the club as they were very accommodating and helpful. In England, clubs including Southampton often send players to a local school or hospital as part of their commitment to the community. In return, they are keen to assist players who want to do something in the same spirit.

Over here, clubs and players do a lot of community service or charity work without making a big fuss. It may be because football has become a part of people's daily life throughout its long history but, to me, the fact that clubs have not lost their connection to the local society – despite the impression of the Premier League being a huge global entertainment business – is certainly one of the reasons why I'm in love with English football.

The game itself ended 0–0, but I still think my 100th Premier League game turned out to be a meaningful occasion both for the kids who experienced the whole 90 minutes in the stand, and for myself who spent the entire 90 minutes on the pitch for the 32nd time in the season.

Captain's armband

Since the FA Cup third-round tie against Norwich in January 2017 I started wearing the captain's armband occasionally at Southampton. It's only an armband with 'CAPTAIN' written on it, but it makes its wearer aware of a weight of responsibility and inspires them. Wearing the armband, I feel I need to set a disciplined tone for the other lads to follow.

There are not so many foreign players wearing the captain's armband in England. Although I am the occasional captain partly because I have become one of the older faces at the club, being at a club for a long time or being an older player in the team won't alone allow you to wear the captain's armband. You still have to be recognised as captain material by your manager and teammates. So it makes me proud and delighted every time I have a chance to wear it.

Being the youngest brother of three, people might think I have no leadership qualities, but the truth is that I have almost always been given a captain's role since my elementary-school days in Nagasaki. I wore the captain's armband at Grampus, too, from time to time. The only exception was during my two and a half years at VVV, where I had joined as something of a hired hand from a foreign country.

The reason why I've often been captain may be because I developed an attitude which says, 'I'd rather lead the others myself than follow someone else quietly,' through my childhood surrounded by my two brothers and their friends who were six or seven years older than me. The fact that an age gap has never prevented me from communicating with others from a young age may be another reason, too. After observing from a neutral point of view, I don't hesitate to say something to someone older if I think I need to make my point known, and I don't mind listening to someone younger if I see that his or her opinion must be heard. If this personality trait of mine has made others around me think that I'm captain material, then that's another effect of the 'strength of the youngest'.

Anyway, if my manager and team-mates allow me to wear the captain's armband, I want it to be because they think, 'I want Maya to be our captain,' rather than 'I don't mind having Maya as our captain.'

I always have an image of my ideal captain in my head. In Japan, I think people would see someone earnest, calm and with a broader perspective as an ideal captain, just as Hasebe-san (Makoto Hasebe) is for the Japan national team at the moment.

On the other hand, in the West I'm under the impression that being a strong character can be seen as a good leadership attribute. It's a different personality type from being a role model, but thanks to that character one can lead the group, sometimes even forcefully, when others are at a loss. It's someone who can insist, 'This way!' while all the others are about to head in the wrong direction.

José, who used to be the team captain at Southampton, was a strong character. He would be saying this and that in front of the team even from the pre-match warm-up, displaying his willingness to motivate and lead his team-mates. He was also someone who wasn't afraid to say something to our manager or to those in the suits at the club on our behalf if he felt it was necessary.

In a tight society such as a 'club', older players who might be seen as too assertive by the manager or the board could be in danger of being culled ahead of others. At the same time, people tend to play safe as they grow older, trying to avoid trouble as much as possible. Yet if someone still feels it necessary to express themselves and to lead others passionately and powerfully, I honestly have to admire their strength of character.

As for me as a captain, during the half-time interval I try to say what I think I should to my team-mates as calmly as I can. But on the pitch there are times when I have to raise my voice. Everyone has his particular duty to perform and his own ideas or thinking about how to carry it out. More often than not, telling someone to do something doesn't mean it will be understood right away. If I shout, 'You do this here!' at someone, he might shout back, 'But it's like this, so I do that!' at me. But if I think I have to get my point across for the team's sake, I shouldn't shut my mouth in that instance, as these verbal exchanges on the pitch can still have a significant impact on the outcome of the game. I do believe you need to be self-assertive as part of your leadership qualities, especially on the pitch in a foreign country where people around you won't listen to your instructions as passively as you'd expect them to in Japan.

But it doesn't mean I lose my temper with my team-mates during the match. Having said that, I once lost it at VVV when I gave our defensive midfielder an earful for his unresponsive display to my instructions from the back line. I vividly remember the astonished look of my then team-mate, Bobby-san (Robert Cullen), whose facial expression seemed to be saying, 'What the f*** is wrong with you, Maya?!'

In the same way, I don't abuse my captaincy off the pitch, either. I simply can't, even if I want to, to be precise. The team captain is in a position to speak to the referee on behalf of the team on the pitch, but I don't have any say at all among my team-mates about who gets a shirt from an opposition player that is in high demand. It's always first come, first served, when it comes to exchanging a shirt with a popular player after the match.

It was 22 February 2015, two years before I started to wear the captain's armband at Southampton, and we were going to play against Liverpool at home. It was our second Liverpool game of the season, and it was supposed to be the last visit to the St Mary's Stadium by Steven Gerrard as a Liverpool player, since the previous month he had already announced his decision to leave the club at the end of the season.

Gerrard for me was a real different class even among all the Premier League stars, and I'd had huge admiration for him since my teens. In my first meeting with him on the pitch as a Premier League player, I was so much in awe of him that I couldn't actually say anything but was just content shaking his hand after the game.

For his last visit to our home he would be wearing the Merseysiders' away kit in yellow, not the one in the famous red of Liverpool. But it didn't matter at all to me. At that particular time in my third year at Southampton, if winning back my starting place was my goal as a player, getting a shirt from Gerrard was my goal as a Premier League fan. And I just couldn't miss my last chance to achieve that private ambition.

Competition to get Gerrard's shirt was always intense because of his standing. In my first Liverpool game it was

Adam Lallana, who was at Southampton at that time, who got the most coveted prize. Then it was Prowsey, two games in a row. I couldn't get it on the next occasion either, and now had to hope I could be 'fifth time lucky' on his last visit to our home.

But then Gerrard picked up a hamstring injury less than two weeks before our meeting, and my hope was already more or less dashed, because it usually takes a few weeks to come back from that type of injury. I became desperate. I was still a long way off from getting out of the darkness as a player, but felt devastated as a fan as well.

Feeling I just had to get that shirt no matter what it would take, I sent an SOS to my former team-mate, Ricky Lambert, who had moved to Liverpool the previous summer. I sent him a text message, 'I just have to have it. Can you please get a shirt from Gerrard for me?'

I heard nothing from him for more than a week, but when Ricky showed up at St Mary's, his previous home, as a Liverpool player, he approached me with a customary, 'Hey pal!' and then, with a grin, handed me a shirt with 'GERRARD 8' on its back. He'd even had it autographed by the great man. How cool is Ricky?! He was our biggest source of goals when he was at Southampton, but he was still an impressively reliable 'goal-getter' for me even after he left the club. The yellow Liverpool shirt, representing the fulfilment of my very private ambition, has been framed and hung on my wall as a prized possession in my home in Winchester.

Player of the month

In April 2017 I had the honour of receiving the Player of the Month award at Southampton. As a team, it was an OK month for us, with two wins, two draws and two defeats, but having kept three clean sheets in those six games perhaps worked to my advantage. This award, a result of a vote by the supporters, was also pleasing as proof that the positive feeling I'd had throughout the season was right.

By this last phase of the season I felt that the perception about me from outside had begun to change. In my first season at Southampton, even though I was playing regularly as a centre-back, I believe I was only recognised as someone doing not too badly for a Japanese defender in his first campaign in the Premier League. Then the perception had become more negative through my second to fourth year here: I was a centre-back who would be not too bad as a back-up, but would be a risk as a regular, with a tendency to make simple mistakes. But in my fifth season I felt I had managed to change people's perception about me in a positive direction once again.

For a centre-back to be rated, stability and reliability are prerequisites, especially in the Premier League where not only the media but the spectators, including your own supporters, can be harsh critics. Those prerequisites were the very things people had thought I lacked until the previous season.

I know that when Jack and I started playing as our regular centre-back pair in the mid-season following the departure of José and the injury to Virgil, some sections of the media described us as a 'makeshift' centre-back pair. But it was us two, who have since been in the heart of the defensive line at Southampton, who came close to winning the League Cup and helped the club climb from tenth to eighth in the league table in the second half of the season.

I genuinely meant it when I said, 'Jack deserved to receive this award as well,' on the club's official website upon my receipt of the Player of the Month award. We both changed the perception of us – as back-up players – by finishing the season as regular starters in the team.

Finally, in my fifth season at Southampton, I began to be recognised as a centre-back who can be a regular at a Premier League club, rather than a centre-back who is not bad for a Japanese, as my individual award given by the supporters, i.e. the regular observers of Southampton matches, proved. It also meant that I had reached a milestone in the journey to be a Premier League player that I embarked on when I was a youth-team player in Japan. When I held the crystal trophy for the award, I resolved to work still harder to become a top-level centre-back.

Home away from home

The following 2017/18 season I had my sixth summer at Southampton since originally joining on a three-year contract. Talks for a new contract had begun towards the end of the previous season, and by the time the pre-season was about to start both the club and I had expected a satisfactory conclusion – a new contract with personal terms appropriate to a regular in the team.

I was fortunate, in a way. It was my agent who said to me, 'You really have a knack of getting into the starting 11 at the right time.' When I renewed my contract here for the first time in January 2015, Southampton were short of cover in a centre-back position, with Toby Alderweireld being on the injury list. This time, for the second renewal, the conversation started when I was about to finish the season as a regular starter after José had moved to West Ham a few month earlier and Virgil was on the sidelines surrounded by persistent transfer rumours.

Therefore, it was only natural for the club to be keen to keep me, but at the same time I also thought it would be best for me to stay at Southampton – who I was confident would be trying to make a step up from a mid-table battle to become one of the top-10 regulars in the Premier League – in order to keep on pushing myself to improve further at the top level.

Accordingly, my agent always made a contract renewal at Southampton our first priority during the summer of negotiations. In addition, he had fought hard to improve my terms from those of a first-team squad member to that of a first-team regular. In this country, where the history of football as a professional sport goes back much further than in Japan, whose domestic professional league, the J.League, was only formed in 1992, clubs are extremely adept at contract negotiations, too, so having an agent who can compete on an equal footing was very assuring.

By the time my latest contract, which I signed on my 29th birthday, expires I will be a 31-year-old with eight years' service at Southampton. As an experienced professional footballer, and as a fully grown man, Southampton is the only place I could call my own.

When I came back from Japan national team duty after two international friendlies in France and Belgium in November 2017, I arrived at St Pancras International station on the Eurostar. Those two countries are also in Europe, and Belgium has a similar atmosphere to the Netherlands, where I spent two and a half years. But I still found myself relaxed as soon as my train arrived back in London. Then, on my way to Winchester from there, I really felt, 'I'm coming home.'

By contrast, I now get excited when I go to Japan, as if I'll be on an overseas trip, wondering what is newly popular in the country or what people are really into over there now, and so on.

The place I feel really comfortable is the area on the south coast of England, which Southampton supporters call their 'home'. Hampshire, the county, includes the Southampton bay area where I first lived with my wife, and Winchester where we live now as a family of three with our baby daughter is our adopted home.

All the same, having settled down doesn't mean my challenge is over. My journey as a footballer, which began when I made up my mind to become a professional after moving from Nagasaki to Nagoya inside Japan and has reached the Premier League via the Netherlands, still continues for as long as I strive to be a better player.

In fact, in my sixth season at Southampton the players had to start from scratch yet again in terms of internal competition for a starting place, after Mauricio Pellegrino became our new manager in the summer. As for centre-backs, we started the season with as many as six of us competing, including new arrivals Jan Bednarek and Wesley Hoedt. With the trial-and-error method used under the new regime, the competition for places became even harder during the first half of the season.

If I am to win recognition as a real Premier League-class player, I must produce stable and reliable performances over a much longer timespan than I've managed in previous seasons – especially as I've now reached what people here regard as my peak years in terms of age.

I know that there will still be times when I start a game on the bench, as well as matches where I may only receive six or seven out of ten marks. In the early months of 2018 I even had the misfortune of being kicked out to the sidelines twice on the training ground. First, I suffered a hamstring injury for the first time in my football life, and then shortly after I recovered from it I damaged the ligament in my left knee. And I experienced the fifth managerial change in my time here – Pellegrino was dismissed by the club as our league position had dropped from the mid-table towards the relegation zone since the turn of the year, and Mark Hughes was appointed with only eight league games remaining.

That's why I still need my resilience to help me continue fighting to become better and reach a higher level.

One day the time will come for me to leave Southampton. When it's time, I will be happy if the Saints supporters say, 'He was a good defender,' when remembering my time at the club. 'There was a centre-back named Maya Yoshida, who dreamed of playing in the Premier League as a teenager, then actually became a professional footballer and came to prove himself in the top division in England, and played like a true Premier League defender at Southampton.' If I could be remembered in such a way with respect, it will certainly mean that I fulfilled my ambition, wherever this journey of mine as a footballer takes this samurai from now on.

EPILOGUE

There are multiple reasons, including my good luck, why I have managed to reach where I am today as a Premier League player. Each of those factors has been a vital ingredient of my resilience, so, before the final whistle on this book is blown, I summarise them below.

1. Ability of the youngest

Being able to feel that an age difference doesn't matter, and developing in an environment constantly surrounded by people much older than yourself, will be useful in the meritocratic real world. You are at an advantage to learn through observation since you have both role models and bad examples around you. Not cowering in front of someone older than you, or patronising someone younger, helps to develop your character and can be one of your leadership qualities.

When you are little, you might often taste defeats against someone physically bigger and stronger, but those experiences will toughen you up as well as strengthen your ability to look at a situation from a different angle, such as using your intelligence to gain the upper hand. Competing against someone superior in one way or another helps you to improve and reach a higher level.

2. *English-language ability*

Initially, it's sufficient to get the gist of what someone is saying and to express what you want to say in simple terms. I, for one, in my ninth year living abroad, still struggle occasionally to deliver a talk in a huddle before the game when I wear the captain's armband. (On one occasion I had to shout, 'C'mon!' to finish off, as I realised my team-mates were looking puzzled by my incomprehensible captain's talk …)

Being fluent is not mandatory. Even a defender, who must be able to communicate on the pitch, can still do his job with moderate language skills.

3. *Ability to make decisions*

In the business world, people talk about 'Plan, Do, See'. In my world, 'Do' is to decide. My journey to the Premier League began when I made up my mind to become a professional footballer in my junior high-school days, and then chose to study English at high school.

Once abroad, I chose to socialise and chat with my team-mates as a way to adapt myself to a foreign environment. Left, on more than one occasion, to sort out numerous practical matters in a foreign country, I decided that, as far as possible, I should do things by myself rather than rely on others. If you are not to have any regrets about the way you play your cards, you must take responsibility for your own actions.

4. Ability to adjust

In the tough world of football in a foreign country, your environment can change drastically, even if you stay at the same club. At Southampton, not only were some of the key players picked up by bigger clubs, but managers, too, have been head-hunted or sacked on an almost yearly basis since my arrival. New competitors for a starting place have also appeared year after year.

On the other hand, meeting new people with different characters and qualities can enrich your life and help you improve yourself. You can pick up some of their good habits, and a change of manager can mean a fresh start. If you find you lack something compared to your competitors, you just have to accept that as the reality and strive to improve.

5. Ability to care less

Sometimes, you need to ignore criticism of your inadequacy or mistakes. In the world of professional sport, you can't feel downhearted every time you lose. For a defender, taking criticism on the chin is part of your profession. A defeat or a mistake is something you can develop from. You may not receive high praise after contributing to an uneventful game, but you may be heavily criticised for a single mistake if it leads to a goal being conceded or the game lost. The higher the level, the higher the risk that your mistake will prove costly, and thus the more likely it is for a defender to be jumped upon.

Therefore, I don't really care what is said about my performances in the media. It's better to conserve your energy, and to keep your concentration level high during the game.

6. Ability to repel

Remember, precedents and fixed concepts are there to be broken. Some claimed, for example, that Japan were jinxed and would not be able to qualify for the 2018 World Cup after making a losing start in the AFC third-round qualification. They were wrong. Some, likewise, were adamant that a Japanese centre-back would never be able to cut it abroad. The idea that a boy from the small town of Nagasaki could end up playing in the English Premier League seemed even more improbable to many. Had they been right, I shouldn't be playing for Southampton now. And had I believed them, I wouldn't even have become a professional footballer when I was in Nagoya in the first place.

Feelings of inferiority and pressure, likewise, can be turned back on themselves, to motivate you into bouncing back from them.

7. Ability to respect

Manners are universally important. If you try to embrace a foreign environment, including different languages, cultures and customs, a respectful attitude brings respect from others towards yourself. In the meantime, you should not lose your respect for your own country. If, as a Japanese professional footballer in a foreign country, I misbehave, it might harm the general image of Japanese people, let alone that of the Japanese living in the country in question.

That's part of the reason why I take pains to experience and understand the local culture whenever I'm representing my country on international duty overseas. I don't want anyone to think, 'Japanese people always stay inside their hotel, playing computer games.' Neither players nor supporters should ever be happy with that.

8. *Ability to maintain balance*

Whether it is between a native country and a foreign country, the ideal and the reality, mind and body, offence and defence, or on the pitch and off the pitch, we need to keep a sense of balance. I learned the hard way that, when you are struggling, being too stoic may lead you to distance yourself from others or to be too harsh on yourself. Being able to laugh at yourself can unintentionally make it easier for you to overcome a setback.

In my darkest hours as a Southampton player, teammates occasionally pulled my leg by saying '*Otsukaresama*' (a Japanese catch-all greeting, literally meaning, 'You've worked hard') as they walked past me while I was speaking to the Japanese press in the mixed zone, even though I'd spent the whole 90 minutes on the bench. Part of me flashed a wry grin inwardly, while another part carried on answering the journalists' questions. Both are the real me. In my online blog I show my softer, humorous side; the more serious side comes out in this book. Both are my real faces.

A centre-back blessed with both toughness and subtleness, such as Rio Ferdinand in his playing days, is sometimes referred to here in England as the 'Rolls-Royce of defenders'. If I could get close to that level some day, what should I be called? Maybe a 'Land Cruiser Prado of defenders'? After all, I began my development as a professional player while living in a commuter town for workers at the Toyota Motor Corporation, but compared to the Premier League standard I'm not built like a heavy-duty Land Cruiser so much as like its more nimble mid-sized version, the Prado.

About a month after this book, my first 'foreign book', is due to be published, the World Cup starts in Russia. It will be my second World Cup.

On those Russian pitches I will certainly play against some of the top Premier League players. There will be familiar faces among our Group H opponents. In our first game against Colombia, they have Davinson Sánchez at the back, who has been showing his talents at Tottenham during his first year there. Then, in the Senegal game, I shall face the fleet-footed Liverpool striker, Sadio Mané in Yekaterinburg. In our final game in the group stage, Kamil Grosicki of Hull City, who were in the Premier League until 2017, should be supporting Robert Lewandowski of Bayern Munich in the Polish front line.

If Japan go through to the knockout stage, we may face England or Belgium, who have many Premier League players among their key personnel. There might even be a chance to challenge Argentina, with Lionel Messi of Barcelona and Sergio Agüero, the latter scoring more than 30 goals in all competitions for Manchester City two seasons in a row on his way to the World Cup.

Once the 2018 World Cup is over, another season as a Southampton player will beckon, the dawn of another season for me as a centre-back playing in England. Hopefully it will also lead to more games at international level.

I started as a forward when I was little, then settled into a centre-back's position via defensive midfield. I have come to the Premier League to hone my skills, and strengthen and cultivate myself as a professional centre-back.

Centre-back is not a star role on the pitch. Some even say it's an often unrewarded position. The lead role is usually that of a striker, without whose goals a team cannot win. During the season, the goal of the month will be selected by the media, but we never hear about the tackle of the month or shot-block of the month. Such categories don't exist. More likely, a centre-back will be blamed as someone who cost the game for his team by failing to deal with danger, even if it was his first mistake in the 90 minutes and the last kick of the game.

EPILOGUE

Although an individual can win or lose the game sometimes, football is a team sport in which collective ability matters most. Just as in the business world the backroom staff are just as important as those in more visible roles, so, in a football team, if one position is missing or not working, the team won't function.

My job is as a centre-back. That's the way I live my professional life. I continue to walk that path and have no intention of stopping just yet. I will keep going with my head held high, and with my eyes focused on the road ahead.

Maya Yoshida
Spring 2018, in the final stretch of my sixth year at Southampton

ACKNOWLEDGEMENTS

My immense gratitude goes to my editors and everyone involved in the process of making this book possible. Their words of wisdom and encouragement have carried me to the finishing line, even though I was not a disciplined writer to start with – easily and happily distracted by my baby daughter and then picking up an injury right before the final deadline.

Writing this book has also made me appreciate the presence of the people around me even more. I was just a boy from Nagasaki who, at the age of 12, somehow passed a trial at Nagoya Grampus Eight and started dreaming of becoming a professional footballer. My journey began when I lived in a flat with my oldest brother in Nagoya, where I climbed through the youth ranks and eventually made it to the first team at Grampus, and has now taken me to the Premier League in England – my dream destination as a player since I was a kid. I have met many people along the way and writing this book has given me the opportunity to look back and realise, once again, that I could not be where I am today without their help.

If people see my professional journey as a success so far, it is thanks to the support and guidance from my managers, team-mates, club staff members and my friends, with whom I've shared much laughter on so many occasions. I can honestly say that they all are valuable 'teachers' in my life.

I'm eternally grateful to my parents back in Nagasaki and my two older brothers, who respected my decision to pursue a career in football, despite being the youngest member of the family and only 12 years old.

I'm also grateful to those who believed in me and supported me in getting here: Sef Vergoossen, the first manager I had as a professional player, who kept playing me despite the errors I was making on the pitch; Seigo Narazaki, who rescued the team on numerous occasions with his incredible saves when my own mistakes left us vulnerable; Toshiya Fujita and Kei Yamaguchi, who showed me how a proper professional should be; Mr Hai Berden, the chairman of VVV, who looked after me as a young man living in a foreign country for the first time; Ms Yvonne Flos, whose moral support was invaluable to me when I was sidelined for a long period almost as soon as I joined VVV, and those 'regulars' (they know who I mean) at our gatherings in Düsseldorf.

My sincere thanks also to those who have given me strength to carry on in a challenging new environment since my move to England six years ago, including but not limited to: the lads at Southampton (of course); Hugo for providing countless 'assists' off the pitch; my football agent Joel and the smiling kids at the Football Samurai Academy in London, to whom I'm 'headmaster Yoshida'. My 100th Premier League appearance would have been an even more challenging goal if I hadn't had your backing! I cannot name everyone in this space but I'm certainly not forgetting all my mates who always have time to cheer me on – thank you.

Last but most importantly, my heartfelt thank you with love to my wonderful partner Miku and my precious daughter Ema for being the most important part of my life.

Maya Yoshida